NEW YORK

THE STORY OF A GREAT CITY

Acknowledgments

New York: The Story of a Great City was the product of a fantastic collaborative effort among a group of talented and astonishingly hardworking people at the Museum of the City of New York and Carlton Books. Project Director Kathleen Benson ably co-piloted the organization of the overall production, with the agile assistance of Grace-Yvette Gemmell and the invaluable support of Evelynne Scholnick. Manuscripts and Reference Archivist Lindsay Turley did a tremendous job of researching the images and objects included here and of orchestrating the illustration program, with help from Robbi Siegel and Marah Newman of the Museum's Rights and Reproductions department, and the logistical and organizational support of Director of Collections Access Lacy Schutz. The critical process of digitization was enabled by the Digital Projects team, headed up by Amy DiPasquale; while Director of Collections James W. Tottis's hard work enabled the book to benefit from newly conserved paintings from the collections. The text benefited incalculably from the keen eye of Senior Curatorial Associate Autumn Nyiri. Many thanks as well to the contributing authors, most notably Kathleen Benson, and also including Donald Albrecht, Ryan Carey, Grace-Yvette Gemmell, Steven H. Jaffe, Phyllis Magidson, and Morgen Stevens-Garmon. Special thanks are due to Julia Blaut, Sean Corcoran, Steven H. Jaffe, James Sanders, and James Tottis for their advice, skillful editing, and consultation.

It was a particular pleasure to work with the resourceful and creative team of designers and editors at Carlton Books. Our particular thanks go to Vanessa Daubney and Victoria Marshallsay, whose vision, dedication, and collegiality made all of this possible.

Sarah M..Henry
Deputy Director and Chief Curator
Museum of the City of New York

For Selina Trieff and Bob Henry

METRO BOOKS
New York

An Imprint of Sterling Publishing
1166 Avenue of the Americas
New York NY 10036

METRO BOOKS and the distinctive Metro Books logo are trademarks of Sterling Publishing Co., Inc.

Text © 2011 by Museum of the City of New York

Design © 2011, 2014 by Carlton Books Limited

ISBN 978-1-4351-6103-0

For information about custom editions, special sales, and premium and corporate purchases, please contact Sterling Special Sales at 800-805-5489 or specialsales@sterlingpublishing.com.

Manufactured in China

2 4 6 8 10 9 7 5 3 1

www.sterlingpublishing.com

NEW YORK

THE STORY OF A GREAT CITY

Edited by Sarah M. Henry

METRO BOOKS
New York

PAGE 2 The most famous icon of the City of New York and the symbol of the city as a haven for immigrants, the statue entitled *Liberty Enlightening the World* was a gift to the people of the United States from the people of France to commemorate friendship between the two nations. Completed in 1880 by the sculptor Frédéric-Auguste Bartholdi, it was dedicated in October 1886 on Bedloe's Island (renamed Liberty Island in 1956) in New York Harbor.

PAGE 3 The first Seal of the City of New York was granted by the Duke of York in 1664. Since then, the device has undergone many changes. The seal pictured is the same as the seal in use, except that the date of founding was changed in 1977, by vote of the City Council, from 1664 to 1625, the date then identified as that of the founding of New Amsterdam. The beavers and the windmill vanes pay tribute to the founding industries of the city's economy.

LEFT An illustration from *New York Illustrated*, 1930. It shows "The Great White Way"—otherwise known as Times Square. This description was coined in 1901 by O. J. Gude, the designer of many prominent advertising displays, to describe the new light show that beckoned along Broadway.

OPPOSITE Part of the City's iconic skyline seen from New Jersey. The Empire State Building soars above the other buildings in New York's midtown Manhattan.

Contents

Introduction

What did it take to make a great city? As the pages of this book attest, New York grew over the course of its almost 400-year history from a small colony of a few hundred Native Americans, Europeans, and Africans to become one of history's most important urban centers. Today, New York City is not only the largest city in the United States, but also the densest and most diverse. Although it was only briefly the nation's political capital, it grew to become its most important port; its center of business and finance; its largest industrial center; its cultural capital; and, perhaps most famously, the point of arrival for generations of immigrants.

New York's trajectory has been shaped by many factors, starting with its location on one of the world's great natural harbors and on the banks of a majestic river. But ambitious New Yorkers transformed that landscape using many tools—landfill to shape its shorelines, a visionary gridded street plan, a marvel of a gravity-fed water system, and a remarkable 363-mile long canal that made New York the lynchpin connecting the wealth and markets of Europe with the breadbasket of the Midwest. Beginning in the middle of the nineteenth century, they developed even bigger plans to provide amenities that would make New York a world-class city: creating now world-famous parks and cultural institutions; growing the city by consolidating the surrounding counties into a five-borough metropolis; linking their city of islands with bridges, tunnels, and a massive subway system; and ultimately equipping it with record-breaking skyscrapers, a road system for cars, vast areas of residential development in all of the boroughs, the nation's first public housing projects, and a massive park system. In the twenty-first century, the wheels keep turning, with the focus of planning on sustainability and how to accommodate a projected one million more residents by 2030.

But of course the city owes its vitality not only to its manmade environment, but to the work, energy, and creativity of its people. Its diverse citizens give the city its character—its distinctiveness as a "city of neighborhoods," its lively street culture, its in-your-face attitude, its restless striving, its often combative politics. Millions of immigrants and migrants have poured into its streets over the course of almost four centuries and have literally built the city. It was also they who made its multifaceted cultures, not only through their own energy, but through their creative and sometimes contentious interactions with each other. Today, New York's immigrants and population are more diverse than ever, and New Yorkers continue to reinvent their city in ways unimaginable a century ago, constantly renewing it as one of the most exciting places on earth.

The Museum of the City of New York is dedicated to exploring the very qualities that define this great city: diversity, opportunity, and perpetual transformation. We are delighted to shed new light on that history in *New York: The Story of a Great City* through the Museum's rich collections of prints, photographs, and paintings, as well as selections from its historical ephemera, costume, and decorative arts collections. The story of New York never fails to astonish, and we invite you to explore it through these pages, at the Museum, and online at collections.mcny.org.

Susan Henshaw Jones
Ronay Menschel Director, Museum of the City of New York

LEFT Samuel H. Gottscho took this photograph from the roof of the St. George Hotel in downtown Brooklyn. The view is facing northwest towards the East River, the Brooklyn Bridge, the Manhattan Bridge, and midtown Manhattan. The Empire State Building is at center, and the Chrysler Building at the right.

New Amsterdam and New York

The area that is New York City was originally inhabited by people of the Algonquian language group, who called themselves the Lenape (or the Lenni Lenape, meaning "true people"). Several hundred of them had seasonal villages and camps throughout today's five boroughs; they farmed, fished, and hunted, they cleared the land through use of controlled fires, and they called themselves, their settlements, and the lands they used by names that resonate down through the centuries—Canarsee, Gowanus, Maspeth, Raritan, and Mannahatta (Island of many hills).

The first Europeans came by accident, looking for a westerly route to the riches of India, China, and the Spice Islands. The Italian explorer Giovanni da Verazzano, under the employ of the French crown, sailed into today's New York Bay in 1524 while searching the East Coast of North America for a route to the Pacific Ocean. Eighty-five years later, the English explorer Henry Hudson disobeyed the orders of his Dutch employers, who had instructed him to

sail northeastward along the northern coast of Russia, instead following his hunch that the most direct course to the Pacific was westward. He entered New York Bay in September 1609, and sailed up the river that would one day bear his name, reaching as far as present-day Albany before concluding that he had not found the route he sought.

Hudson's reports of an abundant population of beavers and other fur-bearing animals, as well as of many Indians willing to trade, sparked the interest of his Dutch employers. They soon established trading posts on Manhattan and upriver. Eventually, the Dutch West India Company (WIC), under charter from the Dutch government, colonized the region as a defensive measure against the English, who were busily laying claim to the surrounding territories. New Netherland, the name for the territory the Dutch claimed—an area roughly between the Connecticut River to the north and the Delaware River to the south—began to appear on Dutch maps.

Director Peter Minuit reported purchasing the island of Manhattan from the Native Americans for goods worth 60 guilders in 1626 (the amount was mythologized as 24 dollars by historians some 300 years later), and soon what began as a company trading post developed into the town of New Amsterdam.

Neither town nor colony flourished until after 1640, when the WIC finally gave up its monopoly on the fur trade and permitted the entrepreneurial settlers to go into business for themselves. The inhabitants were a diverse lot from the first, including not only the Dutch, but also Walloons and Huguenots, Swedes, and English, and as early as 1626, a small but growing number of African slaves.

By 1643, according to a French missionary who visited the town, 18 different languages could be heard on the streets of tiny New Amsterdam. Director General Petrus Stuyvesant, who took control in 1647 and who oversaw the growth of the colony after the disastrous conflict with the Indians known as General Kieft's War saw religious diversity as a threat to order and civic unity, and tried to exclude Jews and Quakers. Ultimately, however, his employers back in the Dutch

OPPOSITE A nineteenth-century imagining of what a Lenape settlement would have looked like before the arrival of Henry Hudson. Native people living in seasonal camps, probably clustered in today's Inwood, Upper East Side, and Lower Manhattan.

RIGHT The donor of this seventeenth-century Dutch woman's cap traces its history to New Amsterdam, to the family of Barent Jacobsz Cool (b. 1610), who was a laborer in the weigh-house and a porter in the public store of the town.

BELOW Asher B. Durand's 1838 painting *Dance on the Battery in the Presence of Peter Stuyvesant* depicts the staunchly Calvinist Director General, with his peg leg, looking scandalized at the goings-on as a young woman recently arrived from the Netherlands shows off her short petticoats.

Republic forced him to accept more diversity than he would have chosen.

In its heterogeneity, in its active marketplaces, and in its contentious politics, New Amsterdam revealed a common spirit with the American city it would become. However, by 1664, this Dutch colony, situated between New England and Virginia, was a thorn in the side of the English. During a time of peace between the Anglo-Dutch wars of 1652–54 and 1665–67, the citizens of New Amsterdam were surprised by a fleet of four English warships sailing into the harbor. Unprepared and urged by his councilors not to fight, Stuyvesant surrendered the colony to the English without a shot being fired. The Dutch briefly retook the colony in 1667 but ceded it back to the British by the 1674 Treaty of Westminster, which brought the Third Anglo-Dutch War to an end, and with it the Dutch claim in North America.

ABOVE Director General Petrus Stuyvesant's signature dominates this 1664 patent for a parcel of land in Brooklyn granted to Thomas Lambertse of Pearl Street.

OPPOSITE In 1660, Jacques Cortelyou, the surveyor general of the province of New Netherland, drew up a detailed plan of New Amsterdam for the directors of the Dutch West India Company. This map is based on a 1667 copy that was discovered in Italy almost 250 years later, and it is called the "Castello Plan," after the Villa Castello, where it was found. The wall after which Wall Street was named can be seen on the north end of town at the right edge of the map; at the left is Fort Amsterdam and the settlement's windmill.

Under English rule, the colony, renamed New York in honor of the Duke of York, brother of King James II, and the town, also renamed New York, continued on much as they had before. The diverse population gradually learned English and adapted to English law, and the entrepreneurs among them prospered after Parliament passed the 1678 Bolting Act, which gave New York merchants the exclusive right to mill grain as well as to build ships to transport flour and meal to the other colonies and to England. (The official seal of the City of New York features two beavers, a nod to its first commercial venture, as well as two flour barrels and the vanes of a windmill as a testament to the source of the colony's wealth under the English.)

New York was such a favored colony, in fact, that while the populations of the surrounding English territories chafed against the rule of the crown there was little sympathy among New Yorkers. New York was a Loyalist town and would spend much of the American War of Independence under English occupation.

GOTHAM AND ITS KNICKER-BOCKERS

New York has had many nicknames—the Big Apple, Fun City, the Empire City. But none is more enduring or evocative than "Gotham." Originally an insult (in English folklore, "Gotham" was a town of fools, albeit "wise fools"), the name was applied to New York by, among others, the satirist Washington Irving. It was taken up with pride by New Yorkers, evidently immune to the original disdain behind it.

Irving was also responsible for another enduring nickname—Knickerbocker (meaning a quintessential New Yorker—now seen in the name of the New York Knicks basketball team and elsewhere). "Knickerbocker" referred to Diedrich Knickerbocker, the mythical "historian" who narrated Irving's satirical 1821 book *A History of New York from the Beginning of the World to the End of the Dutch Dynasty*. Knickerbocker's depictions of Dutch New York created a mythical past that has continued to shape popular beliefs about life in New Amsterdam.

New York in the Revolution

On the eve of the Revolutionary crisis, New York City's ties to England were strong. In fact, throughout the American Revolution, many of the city's residents, loyal to England, opposed General George Washington and sided with King George III against the revolutionaries. Given that—and the fact that New York's harbor was of great strategic importance—it should be no surprise that the British military leaders chose an invasion of New York as the starting point for their quest to reclaim their rebellious colonies.

It was certainly no surprise to General Washington, who dispatched regiments from Massachusetts to New York City. On April 13, 1776, after the British had evacuated Boston, Washington arrived in New York with additional troops, believing that it would be the next target of British attack. He was right. At the end of June, some 9,000 British troops, under the command of General Sir William Howe, arrived at New York Harbor. On July 2, they took Staten Island. That same day, in Philadelphia, New York was the only colony to abstain from voting for independence.

Nevertheless, events in New York soon turned many Tories (Loyalists) into Patriots. On July 9, New York's Provisional Congress approved the Declaration of Independence. As the document was read at the head of each brigade of the American army in or near the city that same day, exuberant Patriots ran through the streets, tearing down royal coats of arms wherever they were displayed. Others toppled the gilded lead equestrian statue of George III mounted on a stone pedestal at Bowling Green, decapitated the figure, and shipped both the lead rider and his lead horse via oxcart to Connecticut to be melted down into bullets. As the oxcart made its way toward Litchfield, Connecticut, Loyalists stole some of the load and scattered the pieces in a swamp near the town of Wilton. (In 1972, a Wilton resident wielding a metal detector unearthed a fragment of the statue; that fragment is now in the collection of the Museum of the City of New York.)

July and early August saw the arrival of the British fleet, under Admiral Lord Richard Howe. The fleet carried some 13,000 additional troops, bringing British strength up to 24,000 soldiers. Washington sent most of his own troops, numbering several thousand, to Brooklyn to fortify Brooklyn Heights, but Admiral Howe shifted many of his regiments across the bay and, on August 27, challenged Washington in the Battle of Long Island (also known as the Battle of Brooklyn). The American army was defeated, and all that saved Washington was Howe's failure to pursue him. During the night of August 29, under cover of

ABOVE In this classic portrait of George Washington, attributed to William Winstanley, Washington is depicted as commander of the American forces in the Revolutionary War.

OPPOSITE, ABOVE An 1859 depiction of revolutionaries pulling down the statue of George III at Bowling Green in Lower Manhattan on July 9, 1776. Days later, the British fleet sailed into the Port of New York. They quickly retook the city and did not leave until seven years later, with the end of the war.

OPPOSITE, BELOW This Currier & Ives print depicts the triumphant return of George Washington to New York City hours after the evacuation of the British troops on November 25, 1783. Celebrations included banquets, fireworks, and illuminations. Spirits were high, but the city itself was badly damaged—much of it destroyed by fire, many of its inhabitants living in shanties, the trading foundation of its economy decimated.

dense fog, Washington managed to move his entire force across the East River to Manhattan.

Two weeks later, Washington decided to evacuate New York City. The American withdrawal to the hills of northern Manhattan was underway when the British landed at Kip's Bay on September 15. Washington retreated to Harlem Heights. General Howe launched an attack on the American troops there the following day, but the Americans managed to repulse it. In an effort to determine Howe's next moves, Washington sent a young officer named Nathan Hale into the city. Hale, a recent graduate of Yale College, who had been commissioned a captain in the Continental Army, ventured out of uniform to try to obtain information about enemy fortifications. He had the misfortune to be in British-held New York City on the day when the first of a series of devastating fires broke out near Whitehall Slip, which spread up Broadway and Broad Street and moved west to the Hudson River. Several hundred structures,

including Trinity Church, were destroyed. The British believed that Patriots had deliberately caused the fire and so rounded up as many people for questioning as they could. As Hale tried to make his way back to the American forces, he was caught up in the dragnet. Taken before General William Howe at the British headquarters in the Beekman Mansion, which stood on the corner of what is now First Avenue and 51st Street, Hale admitted to spying and was hanged the following day. Hale's purported last statement, "I regret that I have but one life to lose for my country," made him a posthumous hero.

In mid-October, Washington retreated to White Plains with the bulk of his forces. He left fewer than 3,000 troops to hold Fort Washington at what is now 184th Street. The British attacked the fort in November and took all surviving Americans prisoner. The whole of the island of Manhattan was now in the hands of the British. The loss of New York City to the British army was one of George Washington's greatest defeats.

New York City remained under British occupation and martial law for the duration of the war—the next seven years. Loyalists from the surrounding area and other colonies flocked to the city, as did escaped slaves seeking the freedom that the British had promised them for going over to the king's side. The British did not leave until November 25, 1783, following the signing of the Treaty of Paris. That same day, General Washington, escorted by the New York governor, George Clinton, returned to Manhattan in triumph. He found a devastated city whose population was half of what it had been before the war. Many citizens had fled, and the remaining residents were impoverished and malnourished. Two great fires had destroyed many of the city's buildings. General Washington offered encouragement and hope for the city's future: "May the tranquility of your City be perpetual; May the Ruins be repaired; Commerce flourish; Science be fostered, and all the civic and social virtues be cherished in the same illustrious manner, which formerly reflected so much credit on the inhabitants of New York …."

EVACUATION DAY

On November 25, 1783, the joyous day of the British evacuation from New York, a resentful Redcoat nailed the British flag to the top of the flagpole at Fort George. To prevent the Americans from taking the flag down, he also removed the climbing cleats and, for good measure, greased the pole. The Americans wasted no time in countering this mean-spirited act. Men came forward with cleats and nails, and a sailor boy ascended the flagstaff, nailing on the cleats as he went up. When he had managed to replace the Union Jack with the Stars and Stripes, three cheers went up from the crowd and nearby troops fired a 13-round salute.

Evacuation Day remained a civic holiday in New York for more than 100 years, and the celebrations at the Battery typically featured a greased-pole climbing contest in commemoration of the event.

LEFT A painting of Evacuation Day, November 25, 1783. The American flag is attached to the flagpole as the British flag (its colors wrongly depicted, in a moment of artistic license) falls to the ground, before the last British ships—bearing British troops and refugee freed slaves and Loyalists—are even out of sight of the crowds in Battery Park.

Rising Economic Power

In the decades following the American Revolution, New York became the new nation's great emporium of commerce and finance. When, in 1789, George Washington was sworn in as president on the balcony of Federal Hall, and New York City briefly became the federal capital, Philadelphia remained the leading port city and population hub. But the future belonged to New York. By 1797, New York had surpassed Philadelphia as the nation's leading seaport, and by 1810, it was the most populous city. Merchants took advantage of the wars of the French Revolutionary and Napoleonic eras to expand their overseas trade as "neutral carriers" at the expense of their English and French shipping rivals. After Britain had retaliated against American cargo ships, President Jefferson's 1807 Embargo on foreign trade backfired, paralyzing the urban economy. "The streets near the waterside were almost deserted," an observer noted, "[and] the grass had begun to grow upon the wharfs …." Yet the city's economy bounced back, entering an era of unprecedented expansion and prosperity following the War of 1812.

As the first Secretary of the Treasury (1789–95), New Yorker Alexander Hamilton had envisioned much of this urban growth. Hamilton's idea of a strong federal union supported by a central bank, import duties, and investment in government securities favored the development of an urban economy based on maritime trade and finance. In harmony with Hamilton's vision, traders gathered under a buttonwood tree on Wall Street in 1792 to found the association that would later become the New York Stock Exchange. By the 1830s and 1840s, as American and European investors increasingly relied on Manhattan investment houses for stocks and bonds in canal companies, state governments, and railroads, "Wall Street" entered the transatlantic vocabulary as shorthand for New York's emerging role as the financial dynamo of the American economy.

Ethnic diversity and social tensions went hand in hand with economic expansion. New York State did not abolish slavery until 1827; after that date, the city's free African-American population remained burdened by racism and discrimination. Meanwhile, European immigrants—Irish, Germans, Britons—arrived in numbers that swelled the city's labor force and gave a public face to poverty in overcrowded working-class neighborhoods such as Five Points and Bancker Street. By 1847, the former mayor, Philip Hone, could lament that New York was becoming like "the large cities of Europe," blighted by "the two extremes of costly luxury ... and hopeless destitution." Crime, riots, and street violence obscured the more stable community and domestic life created by many immigrants.

ABOVE Spring blossoms in Battery Park at the southern tip of the financial district of Lower Manhattan, New York City. Photographed in May 2008.

LEFT This view of Liberty Street, from Broadway to Greenwich Street, was made in 1855 and shows the new construction that had widened the street and swept away the remnants of Dutch colonial architecture. The hubbub on the streets and the array of signs attest to the lively commercial life of the area.

Population growth also literally pushed on the city's traditional boundaries. When construction of a new City Hall began in 1803, the Common Council paid to clad the back of the building with brownstone rather than marble, evidently assuming that the city's outskirts would remain sparsely settled for years to come. Others, however, anticipated rapid and far-reaching growth up the length of the island of Manhattan. A state commission surveyed the island in 1808–11, imposing a future "grid" of rectilinear streets and avenues to facilitate health, transit, trade, and real estate transactions even as it effaced the island's natural landscape of hills, valleys, ponds, and streams. Such planning proved prescient. By 1823, New York City had absorbed the old suburb of Greenwich Village, and by 1855 the city's settled outskirts stretched north to 34th Street and beyond. Meanwhile, buoyed by the city's economy, suburbs sprouted across the East River in Brooklyn and Williamsburg, and across the Hudson in Jersey City and Hoboken.

The booming metropolis fostered a vibrant cultural life and a new world of urban spectacle. In Broadway hotels, international tourists mingled with Southern traders in town to buy textiles from Pearl Street's dry goods importers. Battery Park and City Hall Park were used for public "promenades" by visitors and natives alike. New York was also becoming a city of ideas, a place where Washington Irving brainstormed with other writers at the Shakespeare Tavern, and where a New York University professor, Samuel F. B. Morse, pioneered breakthroughs in telegraphy and photography. Special events, such as the arrival of the Revolutionary hero Marquis de Lafayette in 1824, and the Grand Celebration marking the completion of the Erie Canal in 1825, became occasions for elaborate parades and the mass expression of local pride. New York also became the nation's dominant city for publishing and journalism. In the 1830s and 1840s, Benjamin Day of the *Sun*, James Gordon Bennett of the *Herald*, and Horace Greeley of the *Tribune* created the

ABOVE Artist Anthony Imbert painted this canvas in 1825, the same year as the celebration of the opening of the Erie Canal that it depicts. Nearly 20,000 people gathered on the shoreline to watch the flotilla of watercraft parading through the Harbor to greet the *Seneca Chief*, the first canal boat to travel the full span of the 400-mile waterway.

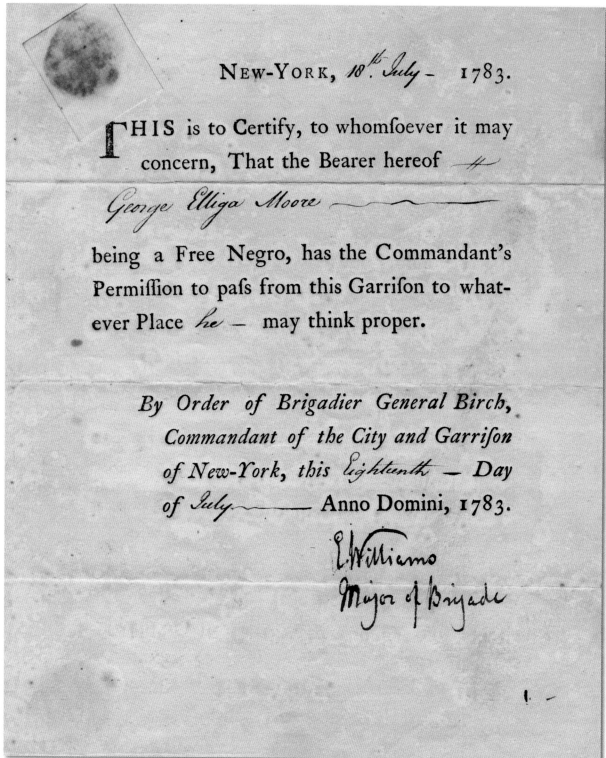

NEW-YORK, 18th July — 1783.

THIS is to Certify, to whomſoever it may concern, That the Bearer hereof —

George Elliga Moore —

being a Free Negro, has the Commandant's Permiſſion to paſs from this Garriſon to whatever Place *he* — may think proper.

By Order of Brigadier General Birch, Commandant of the City and Garriſon of New-York, this *Eighteenth* — Day of *July* —— Anno Domini, 1783.

E. Williams
Major of Brigade

RIGHT During the time of slavery, both enslaved and free Africans and African Americans were required to carry travel passes. This pass, signed by the commandant of the City and Garrison of New-York, permitted a free Negro named George Elliga Moore to depart the garrison on July 18, 1783, in the waning days of the British occupation of New York City during the American Revolution.

"penny press," reinventing the daily newspaper as an inexpensive vehicle of crime news, society reporting, sports, and political opinion for an urban readership of tens of thousands.

By 1853, when the Crystal Palace Exhibition (erected on the current site of Bryant Park) showcased the achievements of American and European manufacturers, inventors, and artists, New York could truly claim to be the "Empire City," the nation's headquarters for finance, industry, trade, and civilization. No wonder that the poet and newspaperman Walt Whitman could describe his city as "the great place of the western continent, the heart, the brain, the focus, the main spring, the pinnacle, the extremity, the no more beyond, of the New World."

Painted on the spot by
Nicolino Calyo

THE GREAT FIRE OF 1835

On the evening of December 16, 1835, a fire, probably caused by a leaking gas pipe, broke out in an office on Merchant Street in Lower Manhattan. The flames quickly spread to dozens of adjoining counting houses and warehouses. Unable to open frozen hydrants, firemen tried to pump water from the East River, but the fire outran their efforts. By the following morning, 674 buildings lay in ruins, including the majestic Merchants' Exchange on Wall Street, a meeting place for businessmen since 1827. Although only two people died in the fire—testimony to the desertion of the commercial district after work hours—property losses were tallied at about $20 million.

Unequaled in scope, the Great Fire of 1835 overnight swept away many of the city's oldest buildings and left merchants and brokers reeling in disbelief. Philip Hone described it as "the most awful calamity which has ever visited these United States." Yet a resurgent business district, including a rebuilt Merchants' Exchange, rose like a phoenix from the ashes. A year later Hone reported that, "As an evidence of the prosperity of the city, the whole is rebuilt with more splendor than before." But destruction remained an omnipresent threat: over 2,500 fires broke out in the city between 1837 and 1848 alone.

LEFT Artist Nicolino Calyo, an immigrant from Italy, had moved to New York from Baltimore only months before the Great Fire of 1835. He made a name for himself for a series of gouaches depicting the drama and devastation of the disaster—here, the burning of the Merchants' Exchange.

The Port of New York

In September 1609, Robert Juet, an officer on Henry Hudson's *Halve Maen*, described the vessel's landfall in "a very good harbour ... pleasant with grass and flowers, and goodly trees." Over the ensuing centuries, New York became the nation's (and then the world's) busiest harbor. The site was blessed with great natural advantages: an upper bay sheltered from ocean storms and fogs, abundant deep anchorages, access to the northern wilderness via the Hudson River and to Long Island Sound through the East River, and a shoreline that ultimately provided 578 miles of waterfront. Settlers and mariners built on this natural base, constructing piers and warehouses and pushing out shorelines with landfill. Every important factor in the city's history—from trade and immigration to finance, industry, and cultural life—would be tied to New York's identity as a port.

Under Dutch and English rule, merchants and seamen developed trade routes across the Atlantic and Caribbean, trading Hudson Valley furs, lumber, grain, and flour for European manufacturing, West Indian sugar, and African slaves. The East River waterfront became the colonial port's focal point for business. Following the American Revolution, New York merchants pioneered the China trade, dominated the South's cotton export trade, and shipped American raw goods to Liverpool and other European ports and brought back hardware, textiles, luxury goods, and immigrants. The Erie Canal (constructed 1817–25 under the auspices of Governor De Witt Clinton),

which cut across New York State for 363 miles from the Hudson River to Lake Erie, made New York the commanding port for trade between the East Coast and the Midwest, clinching the city's primacy in America's commercial economy.

Such trade shaped every aspect of the city's daily life. At waterfront markets and slips (narrow inlets between city blocks), laborers and clerks unloaded boatloads of fruit, meat, fish, and other foodstuffs for sale to retailers and consumers. In shipyards at Corlears Hook, Williamsburg, and Greenpoint, shipwrights turned out a wide array of sloops, schooners, three-masted ships, and other vessels for commercial and recreational use. Brooklyn naval architect George Steers designed the yacht *America*, in 1851 the winner of what would become known as the America's Cup. More crucially, oceangoing vessels remained the workhorses of the city's economy. Maritime trade provided the profits that drove the city's labor and real estate markets, financial growth, cultural patronage, and philanthropy. From the 1820s, revenues from the New York customhouse paid most of the federal government's budget; port revenues also allowed Governor De Witt Clinton to keep state taxes low.

Meanwhile, New Yorkers also pioneered the Age of Steam. Inventor Robert Fulton launched his first steamboat from Manhattan to Albany in 1807; by 1815, steam-powered ferries crossing the East River and Hudson River enabled commuters to develop the suburbs

of Brooklyn, Hoboken, and Jersey City. The first transatlantic steamships, the *Sirius* and the *Great Western*, arrived in New York from England in 1838, inaugurating a new era in ocean travel and spelling the eventual demise of sailing vessels. The steamship also transformed immigration, cutting the transatlantic passage in steerage (the third-class quarters below decks) from about one month to two weeks, and providing transport for the great waves of late nineteenth-century and early twentieth-century immigrants to New York from Southern and Eastern Europe. At the other end of the social scale, affluent travelers sailed in style aboard luxury ocean liners, "floating hotels" that berthed at West Side piers. By the Second World War, New York was the world's busiest port. "In the remotest corner of the world the image of a ship entering New York harbor, into the shadow of skyscrapers, will strike

ABOVE Berenice Abbott (1898– 1991) captured New York's evolving waterfront as part of her Depression-era series *Changing New York*.

LEFT A magnificent full-rigged ship adorns this creamware jug, inscribed "Sacred to the Memory of George Washington."

OPPOSITE The George Washington Bridge, shown here in an image taken by Samuel Gottscho only a year after it opened in 1931, is the only bridge crossing between New Jersey and New York City, and only the second vehicular crossing built (after the Holland Tunnel).

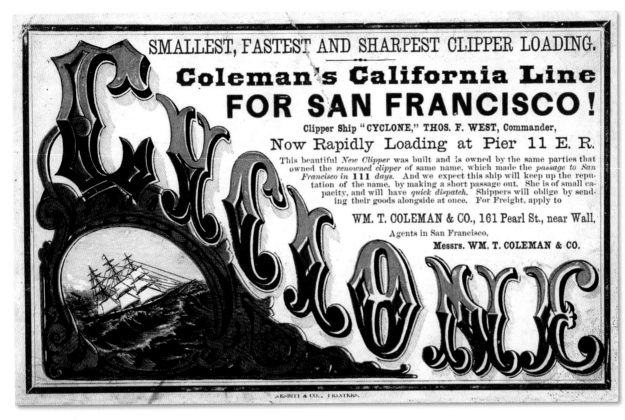

SMALLEST, FASTEST AND SHARPEST CLIPPER LOADING.

Coleman's California Line
FOR SAN FRANCISCO!

Clipper Ship "CYCLONE," THOS. F. WEST, Commander,

Now Rapidly Loading at Pier 11 E. R.

This beautiful *New Clipper* was built and is owned by the same parties that owned the *renowned clipper* of same name, which made the *passage to San Francisco in 111 days*. And we expect this ship will keep up the reputation of the name, by making a short passage out. She is of small capacity, and will have *quick dispatch*. Shippers will oblige by sending their goods alongside at once. For Freight, apply to

WM. T. COLEMAN & CO., 161 Pearl St., near Wall.

Agents in San Francisco,

Messrs. WM. T. COLEMAN & CO.

NESBITT & CO., PRINTERS.

a chord of recognition," the writer Jan Morris observed in 1969.

But the late twentieth century brought dislocating changes. During the 1960s, container ships proved too large to dock at city piers, resorting instead to new port facilities built on Newark Bay in New Jersey. Automation drastically cut the supply of jobs for working longshoremen. High labor costs and the difficulty of moving cargoes from wharves to nearby highways also discouraged maritime business in the city, especially as other American ports competed for a larger share of waterborne trade. Jet travel diminished the demand for ocean liners and immigrant ships. In 1989, New York lost its position as the nation's leading port—a rank it had held since the 1790s—to the port of Los Angeles. By 2004, New York was ranked twentieth. In recent years, however, the Port of New York-New Jersey has enjoyed a renaissance, as traffic in container ships from Asia traveling via the Panama Canal has surged. The maritime identity of the greater port, stretching from the East River to Newark and Elizabeth, New Jersey, has proved hard to kill, even after the passage of four centuries.

OPPOSITE, BELOW Fitz Henry Lane (who usually signed his name "Fitz Hugh") was one of the most celebrated American marine painters of the 19th century. He depicted the clipper ship *Sweepstakes* under full sail in 1853.

BELOW As this Currier & Ives print demonstrates, clipper ships were the queens of the sea, celebrated for their regal beauty as well as for their speed. The *Cosmos* is shown here at full sail.

PACKET AND CLIPPER SHIPS

Much of New York's preeminence in nineteenth-century commerce, travel, and immigration was due to two major innovations: the packet ship and the clipper ship. In 1818, New York merchants commenced the Black Ball Line of "packets," ships that shuttled between New York and Liverpool on a regular schedule. Previously, cargo ships had sailed at the discretion of their captains, regardless of advertised sailing dates. By guaranteeing merchants a predictable schedule, the Black Ball packets and their imitators quickly dominated transatlantic and coastal cargo traffic. In turn, New York's packets became the premier immigration vessels, with thousands—especially Irish fleeing the potato famine (1845–53)—leaving Liverpool in the steerage (below decks) section of packet ships bound for the East River.

The other innovation was the clipper: an unusually narrow, streamlined hull supported a large number of sails, allowing the ship to "clip" along at high speeds en route to the Pacific, California, and China via Cape Horn at the tip of South America. Shipbuilders in Baltimore, East Boston, and Britain, as well as New York, played a role in its genesis. By the late 1840s, clippers enabled South Street merchants such as A. A. Low to hold the lead in importing tea and other Chinese goods into the United States. Clippers also played a dominant role in transporting "Forty-Niners" from New York to the San Francisco gold rush, and set speed records unequaled by any other sailing vessel. For half a century, clippers bound to and from New York engaged the imagination and pride of Americans from coast to coast, until the speed and economy of steamers rendered them obsolete.

Science and Invention

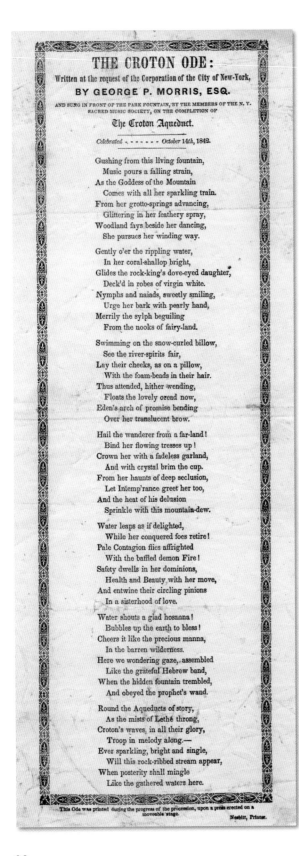

New York has always been a place of new ideas. Its historical intermingling of many cultures, its density, its pursuit of money, and its decidedly American thirst for more, bigger, and better have made the city fertile ground for rapid development and change. To name all of the inventions and scientific breakthroughs that emerged from the laboratories and workshops of New York City would be nearly impossible—they range from the steamboat to radio transmission to photocopying, the telephone, the transistor, the laser, and even toilet paper.

A number of New York's great innovations represent solutions to constraints created by the city's peculiar landscape and location. The relatively small physical size of Manhattan posed challenges for its ever-expanding industry and dense population, and continues to do so. For example, the demand for readily available, sanitary water for drinking and fire prevention led to the city's water supply being revolutionized. Polluted ponds and lakes were built over to accommodate growth; the contamination of well water in Lower Manhattan soon compelled the city to bring in clean water from Brooklyn.

In 1799, Aaron Burr acquired a State charter to develop a waterworks to supply fresh water to Lower Manhattan. Burr's Manhattan Company funded the construction of a water-piping and reservoir system. The charter also included a clause enabling the Manhattan Company to use excess capital to any lawful end and Burr took advantage of this provision

BELOW The Murray Hill Distributing Reservoir, today the site of the New York Public Library at Fifth Avenue and 42nd Street, was part of the Croton Aqueduct system. Opened in 1842, this system brought fresh water from the Croton River in Westchester more than 40 miles to a receiving reservoir on the present site of the Great Lawn in Central Park. From there, the water was piped to distributing reservoirs, such as the one at Murray Hill, to meet the needs of proliferating households and for fire protection.

LEFT This paean to the Croton Aqueduct, the first public water supply for New York City, was sung at the opening celebration on October 14, 1842. That the ode was "printed during the progress of the procession, upon a press erected upon a moveable stage," attests to the significance of the event.

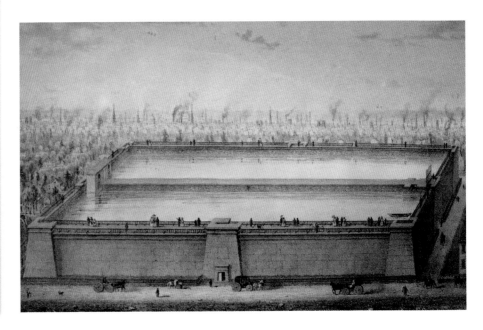

to establish a bank—one of the predecessors of today's JPMorgan Chase. Ultimately, the Manhattan Company's waterworks did not prove adequate to meet demand for potability or firefighting. In 1842, however, the city completed the Croton Reservoir system, an engineering triumph whose 40½-mile aqueduct delivered about 35,000,000 gallons daily from upstate New York, via the force of gravity, to two massive reservoirs constructed in Manhattan. Even today, the supply system that brings water to New York City from many upstate reservoirs is based on the Croton Reservoir, as are many such systems around the world.

Moving people and goods around New York's islands—and 150 miles north to the state capital— was just as challenging. For this reason, many New

Yorkers dedicated themselves to the development of more efficient modes of transportation. Robert Fulton revolutionized travel not only in New York, but worldwide. After the maiden voyage of his steamboat the *North River Steamboat* (later renamed the *Clermont*) in 1807, Fulton noted proudly how he "overtook many sloops and schooners beating to windward, and passed them as if they had been at anchor."

A desire to connect the city's boroughs has been an equally important factor in determining New York's influence on the transportation industry in general. The Brooklyn Bridge, initially designed by German immigrant John Augustus Roebling and completed in 1883, was a feat of engineering genius with a main span of 1,595½ feet. It was one of the first bridges to solve

problems of aerodynamics, with its open truss structure supporting a deck that was six times as strong as Roebling thought necessary. The neo-Gothic structure was the first, and longest, steel-wire suspension bridge in the world until 1903 and just one example of the many answers that New York has provided to the problems of moving its increasing population from point A to point B. Another famous New York inventor, Samuel F. B. Morse, focused his genius on improving the transport of information. When a letter from his dying wife took so long to reach him that he was unable to attend to her, Morse abandoned his career as a painter, at which he had already found great success, and set out to discover a superior way to quickly exchange information over long distances. His single-wire telegraph enabled immediate communication between people in different states, regions, and, eventually, continents. In the 1850s, Morse's invention would lead

LEFT The Grand Opening Celebration for the Brooklyn Bridge was held on May 24, 1883. After a day of speeches, processions, military bands, and salutes, at precisely eight o'clock the first flight of 50 rockets was sent from the center of the bridge. The East River was one big blaze of light for the next hour, the fountains of silver and gold stars having been made possible by the firm of Detwiller and Street, Pyrotechnists.

BELOW Invitation to the opening of the Brooklyn Bridge— originally called the New York and Brooklyn Bridge, May 24, 1883. U.S. President Chester A. Arthur, New York Governor Grover Cleveland, and the mayors of New York and Brooklyn attended the celebration. Sadly, when the bridge was opened to the public a week later, 12 people were trampled after an anonymous shout set off a panic.

to the establishment of the Associated Press and its monopoly on news distribution, which in turn fueled New York's thriving newspaper industry.

Perhaps New York's greatest innovative spirit was Thomas Edison (1847–1931), who worked in New York City as well as in his industrial research laboratory in New Jersey, which acquired over 1,000 US patents. Edison chose to locate his, and America's, first power station in Manhattan, which in 1882 supplied electricity to 59 customers within one square mile for approximately 24 cents per kilowatt hour. Edison's principal competitor in the field of electricity, Nikola Tesla, also made New York his home base, with laboratories located on Fifth Avenue and Houston Street.

New York's coastal geography continually necessitated solutions to unique problems of transportation and infrastructure. Moreover, it

Samuel F. B. Morse (1791–1872) came to New York in 1823 seeking commissions for his paintings. Like many men of his class during the early 1800s, he engaged in a variety of pursuits. Perhaps best known for his invention of the telegraph and the code that bears his name, which revolutionized long-distance communication, in his day Morse was also a distinguished painter, professor, a founder of the National Academy of Design, photographer, and political activist. Of these, the latter is perhaps least widely known. Morse championed the anti-popery cause and supported anti-Catholic agitation. On this platform, he ran an unsuccessful campaign as mayoral candidate, on the anti-immigrant Native American ticket, in 1836.

positioned the city as particularly receptive to new ideas from around the world. In turn, both of these aspects energized and shaped the city's creative culture. Edison, for example, would not have developed the modern motion-picture system if not for the contribution of Englishman Eadweard Muybridge; Morse, who brought photography to America, learned the basics of the new art and science from Frenchman Louis Daguerre; Fulton, with his patron, New Yorker Robert Livingston, spent time in France, where he honed his nautical creativity by developing the first working submarine. And New York's Crystal Palace Exhibition of 1853, a celebration of science and industry, was an effort to recreate the success of London's venture of two years before.

In the twentieth and twenty-first centuries, New York's scientific and technological breakthroughs have been nurtured by the massive brainpower represented in the city's colleges, universities, hospitals, and museums, as well as in the private sector. Columbia University (then known as King's College) provided the first scientific training in the colonial city and has continued to produce Nobel-winning scientists and countless discoveries and inventions. Today the city is home to scores of research institutions, including the massive publicly-funded City University of New York, the private New York University, and Rockefeller University, which is entirely dedicated to biomedical research. And the concentration of Internet and new media companies in Silicon Alley has ushered in many venture capitalist opportunities in New York's dot-com industry.

ABOVE The Crystal Palace, on the site of today's Bryant Park, was built in 1853 as the location of the "Exhibition of the Industry of All Nations"—America's first World's Fair. Modeled on the Great Exhibition at the Crystal Palace in London just two years earlier, it was adjacent to the 42nd Street reservoir visible on the left of this print by John Bachmann, and later became the site of displays such as a celebration of the laying of the first transatlantic cable.

OPPOSITE Thomas Edison, the "Wizard of Menlo Park," with one of his inventions—the phonograph.

RIGHT Samuel Finlay Breese Morse, inventor of the single-wire telegraph system and Morse code.

Coming to America

Inscribed upon the base of the Statue of Liberty, the Emma Lazarus poem proclaims, "Give me your tired, your poor, your huddled masses yearning to breathe free." New York's history as a locus for immigration, however, extends far beyond that of the statue or poem. The quintessential city of immigrants, its character has been made and remade by being the port of first arrival for generations of newcomers to America. Early settlers in New York, including the Dutch and English, sought both economic opportunity in the New World and escape from religious persecution in the Old World. The unwilling immigrants of the period were, of course, the many Africans who were forced to make the journey in captivity. As New York grew into a major city after America gained its independence, immigration occurred in massive waves—Irish, Germans, and Central Europeans in the mid-nineteenth century, and then the "new immigration" of those from Southern and Eastern Europe at the turn of the twentieth.

Having to process such an enormous number of new people on a daily basis forced New York to establish comprehensive centers for immigration. The first of these was Castle Garden, which was earlier a fortification called Castle Clinton (the name to which it has today reverted), and later a popular concert venue, hosting Jenny Lind among others. Beginning in 1855, it became the doorway to New York and the nation. Then in 1892, the federal government moved immigration operations over to Ellis Island in Upper New York Bay,

OPPOSITE, BELOW The majority of immigrants to New York in the late nineteenth and early twentieth centuries traveled steerage class, in crowded, unsanitary conditions. As here, in 1893 on SS *Pennland*, a ship of the Red Star Line (the International Navigation company of Philadelphia), they would take the chance to go out on deck in good weather.

LEFT B'nai Jesherun, New York City's second synagogue, was created in 1825 by members of Congregation Shearith Israel, founded in 1654 as the first Jewish congregation in North America. By 1825, a growing number of Ashkenazi Jews in the city sought to follow their own practices, which were not encouraged in the existing Sephardic congregration.

BELOW Ellis Island National Monument. The island, near the shore of Jersey City, New Jersey, was the first stop in America for generations of immigrants.

off the shore of New Jersey. It was here that Henry James noted the remarkable "drama that goes on, without a pause, day by day and year by year, this visible act of ingurgitation on the part of our body politic and social." Today, two in five Americans can claim that one of their ancestors entered the country through the bustling gates of Ellis Island. During its peak year of operation, 1907, Ellis Island received over a million new arrivals—as many as 11,000 in a single day.

Not everyone found an easier life after having passed through one of New York's immigration centers. Many immigrants lived in squalor, the most extreme examples of which one might have found in an area dubbed Five Points in the era before the Civil War, "which, in respect of filth and wretchedness," Charles Dickens wrote in his *American Notes*, "may be safely backed against Seven Dials, or any other part of famed St. Giles's." And yet, the neighborhood of Five Points was also a classic American example of immigrant energy, creativity, and accomplishment—a place that spawned the invention of

tap dancing, the popularization of prizefighting, and the achievement of political power.

As the complexion—and magnitude—of immigration changed in the late nineteenth and early twentieth centuries, with increasing numbers of Eastern European Jews, Italians, Greeks, Bohemians, Hungarians, and others whose language, culture, and religion were alien to many native New Yorkers, and who crowded the streets and tenements of the Lower East Side and other neighborhoods, a sense of social crisis spread. Among the key figures who championed the rights of poor immigrants in New York was journalist Jacob A. Riis, himself an immigrant from Denmark, who exposed in his book *How the Other Half Lives* the horrid destitution that afflicted many of the city's newcomers. Mary Antin, another advocate for immigrants, sought to eradicate child labor and to redirect the public's ill treatment of immigrants toward "the venal politicians who try to make the immigrant the scapegoat for all the sins of untrammeled capitalism."

Despite the efforts of these champions of the poor, anti-immigrant sentiment prevailed. The Federal Immigration Act of 1924 effectively reduced immigration to a trickle and virtually closed the nation to new groups. The Immigration and Nationality Act of 1952 revised the 1924 law, but it was not until the passage of the Immigration and Nationality Act of 1965 (co-sponsored by New York City Congressman Emanuel Cellar) that US immigration practices were equalized (see page 118, "A Modern Melting Pot").

Castle Garden and Ellis Island having long ago ceased operations, today Kennedy and Newark Liberty International Airports are the modern receiving stations for the newest New Yorkers, who pour into the city, strengthening the New York's unique alloy.

HOW THE OTHER HALF LIVES

Journalist Jacob A. Riis, born in Ribe, Denmark, arrived in New York in 1870, one among thousands of poor, friendless, and unskilled immigrants. In his early years in the city, he frequently spent nights in police station lodging houses, the shelters of last resort in late nineteenth-century New York. As a police reporter from 1877–88, he sought to expose the terrible living conditions in the slums, and, with the invention of flash photography in 1887, he found and employed a powerful new resource to convey the urgent need for reform. Through his 1890 book, *How the Other Half Lives,* and his extensive lecturing, he elevated Americans' awareness of the problems of urban poverty and helped spur successful movements for public playgrounds and for improving legal regulation of urban housing conditions. His collection of photographs is held by the Museum of the City of New York.

LEFT Photojournalist Jacob Riis titled this 1897 image "Yard in Jersey Street (now gone) where Italians lived in the then worst slums."

Politics, New York Style

In New York's early days as a city in the Republic, politics was an activity for the elites. The mayor was appointed by the governor, and only property owners were permitted to vote. As the nation's new capital, New York City was home to George Washington's first presidential inauguration, and the first Congress under the Constitution convened at Federal Hall on Wall Street in March of 1789. However, New Yorkers had not had the chance to vote in the election of the president, because the political leaders had not decided whether to elect or appoint representatives to the Electoral College.

But all of that began to change early in the 1800s. With the advent of the wave of democratic sentiment known as Jacksonian Democracy, New York eliminated property requirements for voting and ushered in an era when all white men in the state could vote, regardless of their wealth. (Ironically, the national spread of the vote to poor white men was accompanied by the

disenfranchisement of landowning women and black men.) The increased importance of the popular vote and the accompanying growth of mass-based political parties galvanized interest in the electoral process. Political parties now campaigned openly and promoted the loyalty of their voters. Electioneering became an ever more public and celebratory activity marked by parading in the streets, often by torchlight.

One driving force in this path to greater political participation was Tammany Hall. Starting out as an exclusive private political club in the late 1780s, complete with the trappings of pseudo-Native American rituals, the Society of St. Tammany eventually grew into a powerful force that effectively controlled the Democratic Party behind the scenes. The tools of Tammany, like those of other political machines, included the securing of votes through patronage, rigorous ward-level political organizing, and, sometimes, outright fraud.

The mastermind behind Tammany's power was

BELOW During the tenure of Irish-born Richard Croker (center, in dark hat), from 1886, disclosures of corruption weakened Tammany Hall. Croker stepped down in 1902.

OPPOSITE, ABOVE This lithograph shows the interior of Tammany Hall on 16th Street, decorated for the national Democratic Party convention on July 4, 1868. Tammany was a key force in Democratic presidential politics from the mid-nineteenth to mid-twentieth century.

OPPOSITE, BELOW The Society of St. Tammany moved to its new headquarters (or "wigwam") on 14th Street near Third Avenue in 1868.

"Honest John" Kelly, the first Irish-American boss, who organized Tammany into an effective vote-getting machine in the 1870s and 1880s. But the most notorious and best remembered of the leaders was "Boss" William M. Tweed, the grand sachem of Tammany from 1863 to 1871. Tweed, a Presbyterian, was the first leader of Tammany to see the possibilities resulting from the spread of the franchise and the potential power of the largely Catholic immigrant voters. He courted their votes with assistance to the poor and rose to power through the ranks from his position as commander of Americus Engine Company Number 6. In the years after the Civil War, Tweed and his collaborators (the "Tweed Ring") oversaw the greatest bilking of the city coffers ever conceived. He parlayed his leadership of Tammany Hall into lucrative opportunities for himself and his friends in such scams as the construction of a courthouse that ended up being the most expensive building ever made to that date—four times the cost of the British Houses of Parliament and twice the cost of the purchase of Alaska in 1867. Tweed ended up dying in jail, but his notoriety lived on.

Despite the rapacious reputation of Tammany, the political machine also played an important role in the city. As a later New York City political boss, George

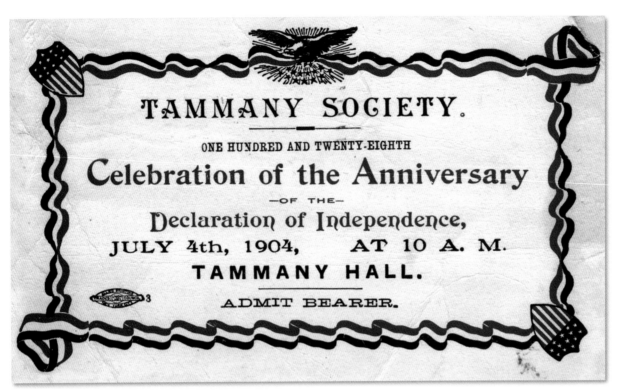

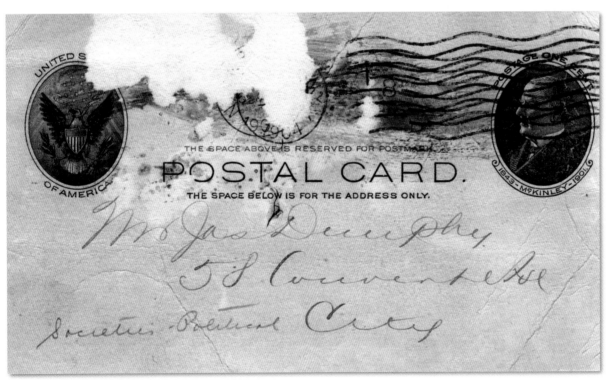

Washington Plunkitt, explained to reporter William Riordan in 1905, the political clubs rendered vital services to the poor—most of them immigrants—at a time when no government agency was providing a social safety net. The political boss could help your cousin through Ellis Island, find your unemployed brother a job, deliver a turkey dinner at Christmas, or bail you out of jail. All that he asked in return was a vote for the Democratic Party.

And he was less likely to steal outright than to commit "honest graft"—using his position and knowledge of city government to make lucrative business and real estate deals for himself even as he looked out for your interests.

Much of the dynamic of New York City politics for a century following the Civil War had to do with expanding or combating the power of the Tammany machine. Some challenges came from the Left (from labor advocates

such as the single tax reformer Henry George); others came from elite reformers who sought to restore order to New York City politics by restraining what they saw as the excesses of the Democrats. But the most profound changes in Tammany politics came from within, in the years just after the First World War, when progressive Tammany politicians themselves began calling for reform, and began proposing the use of government power to bring a form of social welfare to the people. The most notable among them was Al Smith, a product of New York's hardscrabble Lower East Side, who rose through Tammany to become a state assemblyman, sheriff of New York County, president of the Board of Aldermen, governor of New York State, and eventually the first Catholic presidential candidate of a major party.

Smith's presidential ambitions were beaten back in a virulently anti-Catholic and antiurban campaign. But many of his reforms lived on in an anti-Tammany mayoral candidate, Fiorello La Guardia. The Republican Episcopalian son of a Jewish mother and an Italian father, he was a notable exception within a 50-year-long streak of Catholic Democratic mayors in New York City.

LaGuardia—known as the "Little Flower"—served as mayor of New York City during the Great Depression, winning the loyalty of millions, and pioneering a local form of social welfare that was considered to be New York's own "Little New Deal."

Despite La Guardia's popularity, the days of the machine were not over. Another three-term mayor, Robert F. Wagner, expanded the connections among the Democratic Party, Tammany Hall, and the city's labor unions. But by the time he left office in 1965, the city's demographics were changing. The GI Bill and deindustrialization were dismantling the white ethnic working-class base that had supported Tammany throughout the previous century. Wagner turned against Tammany during his third term, and a young Edward I. Koch put a symbolic nail in the coffin of Tammany Hall when he defeated Carmine de Sapio, known as the last Tammany Boss, in an election for Democratic district leader in 1963.

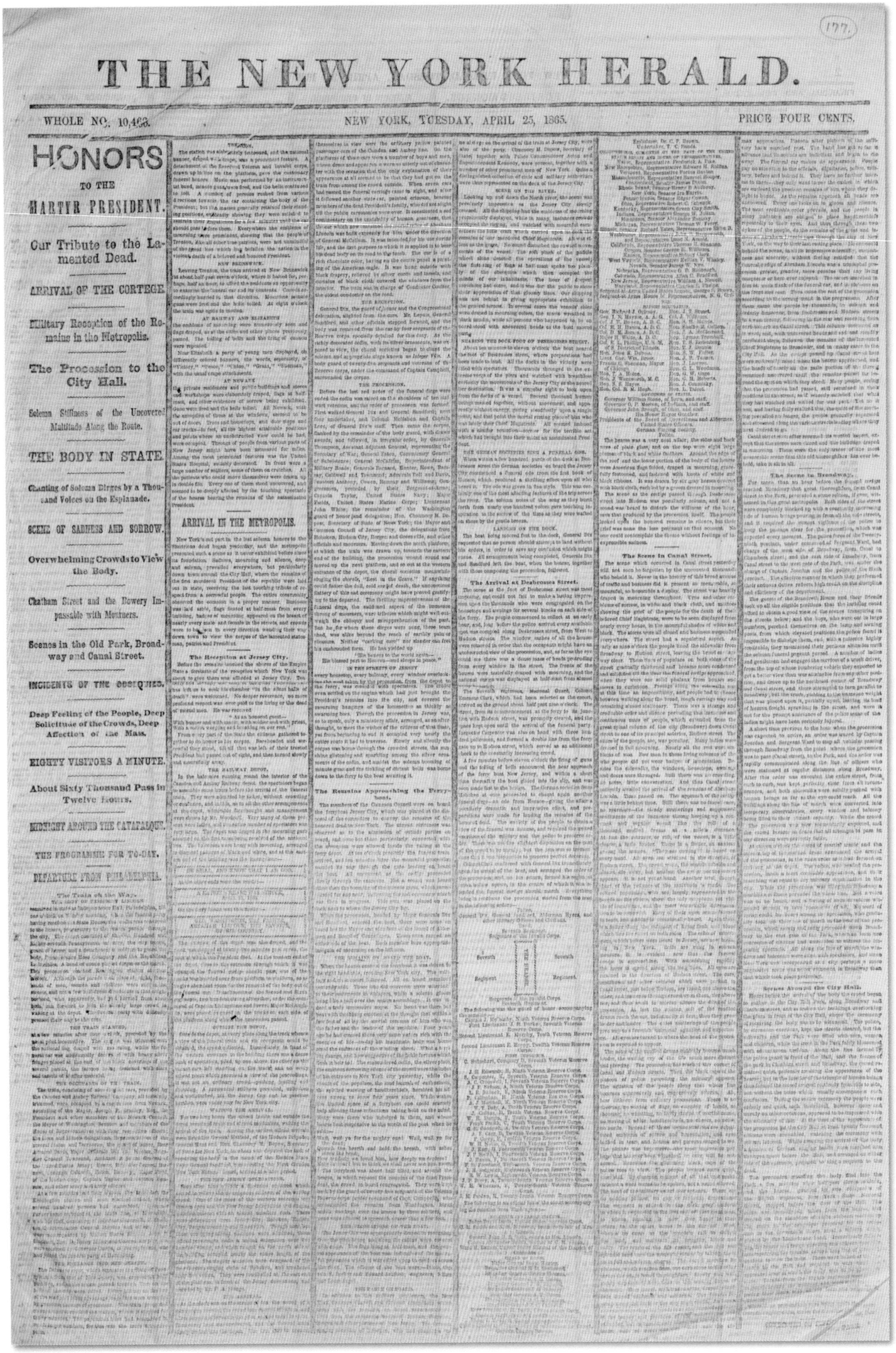

THE NEW YORK HERALD.

WHOLE NO. 10,468.   NEW YORK, TUESDAY, APRIL 25, 1865.   PRICE FOUR CENTS.

HONORS
TO THE
MARTYR PRESIDENT.

Our Tribute to the Lamented Dead.

ARRIVAL OF THE CORTEGE.

Military Reception of the Remains in the Metropolis.

The Procession to the City Hall.

Solemn Stillness of the Uncovered Multitude Along the Route.

THE BODY IN STATE.

Chanting of Solemn Dirges by a Thousand Voices on the Esplanade.

SCENE OF SADNESS AND SORROW.

Overwhelming Crowds to View the Body.

Chatham Street and the Bowery Impassable with Mourners.

Scenes in the Old Park, Broadway and Canal Street.

INCIDENTS OF THE OBSEQUIES.

Deep Feeling of the People, Deep Solicitude of the Crowds, Deep Affection of the Mass.

EIGHTY VISITORS A MINUTE.

About Sixty Thousand Pass in Twelve Hours.

MIDNIGHT AROUND THE CATAFALQUE.

THE PROGRAMME FOR TO-DAY.

DEPARTURE FROM PHILADELPHIA.

[Body text columns illegible]

ARRIVAL IN THE METROPOLIS.

The Reception at Jersey City.

The Railway Depot.

The Remains Approaching the Ferry-boat.

The Arrival at Deabrosses Street.

LEFT Most New Yorkers learned of the 1865 assassination of President Lincoln from daily newspapers such as the New York Herald, which also reported extensively on the city's efforts to honor, in death, the man whom it had failed to support as president. A cortege carrying the slain president's body arrived in the city on April 24, and he lay in state in an open coffin at City Hall until the following day, when the cortege departed the city for Illinois.

HARPER'S WEEKLY.

A JOURNAL OF CIVILIZATION.

Vol. XV.—No. 778.]   NEW YORK, SATURDAY, NOVEMBER 25, 1871.   [WITH A SUPPLEMENT PRICE TEN CENTS.

Entered according to Act of Congress, in the Year 1871, by Harper & Brothers, in the Office of the Librarian of Congress, at Washington.

"WHAT ARE YOU LAUGHING AT? TO THE VICTOR BELONG THE SPOILS."

NAST AND TWEED

William M. Tweed was at the top of his game in early 1871. By the end of the year he had been arrested, and after a hung jury, a prison sentence, a release, a re-arrest, a civil trial, an escape to Spain, and a dramatic capture, he died in jail in 1878. Who or what brought down "Boss" Tweed? In no small part, the arousal of public outrage against him lay with a cartoonist—Thomas Nast, the illustrator who created not only the Democratic donkey and the Republican elephant, but also the Tammany tiger, and the popular visualization of Santa Claus (in his illustrations for Clement Clarke Moore's *The Night Before Christmas*). Nast's political cartoons deftly skewered Tweed and revealed the corruption behind his power, depicting him and his crowd as vultures, as dissolute Roman nobles, and as bloated moneybags. Tweed reportedly complained that the cartoons did him more harm than any newspaper report, because, as he lamented, his uneducated followers could not read the news reports, "But, damn it, they can see the pictures!"

LEFT This cartoon by Thomas Nast appeared on the front page of the November 25, 1871, issue of *Harper's Weekly*, which had waged an energetic anti-Tammany Hall campaign. Nast depicts "Boss" Tweed surrounded by the ruins of his political empire, which had indeed suffered from the constant barrage of criticism from *Harper's* and *The New York Times*. But Nast also depicts Tweed (with a tiger's-head medallion on his chest, the symbol of Tammany Hall) as obese with gluttony, his foot bandaged and elevated to ease the pain of gout, battered but not yet broken.

The Underworld

In the popular imagination and in popular culture, New York City is associated with crime and the underworld, from *The Gangs of New York* to *Law & Order.* While its reputation may be exaggerated, New York's history of crime reflects its role as the largest, densest, most diverse city in the nation. And as the city grew, its underworld in many ways mirrored the city's changing social, economic, and political dynamics.

Street crime first became a major social problem in the years before the Civil War, most visibly in Five Points, the most notorious slum in the city (perhaps in the world), which was located in what is today's Chinatown and courthouse district. Charles Dickens made a pilgrimage to Five Points during his American tour in 1842, and he wrote of the neighborhood, "All that is loathsome, drooping, and decayed is here." Five

BELOW Blackwell's Island (today's Roosevelt Island) lies in the middle of the East River between Manhattan and Queens. The city acquired it in 1828 as the site of a prison (here), an almshouse, a workhouse, and three hospitals. This image from a lantern slide (which cropped the original photograph) was among the first used by Jacob Riis in his 1888 lecture.

OPPOSITE The so-called "Rogue's Gallery" was the Police Department's mug-shot collection. This image (like that below) was among those in the first group of photographs Jacob Riis included in his initial lantern-slide lecture, "How the Other Half Lives and Dies in New York," in 1888. It is probably half of a stereoscope negative (a 3D-effect technique).

CITY OF NEW-YORK, ss.

"William Slater notice to be left at Mr Hawkins' Catharine market of No. *Brooklyn* street, being duly sworn, deposeth and saith, that on the *10* day of *August* 1824 at the *4* Ward of the City of New-York, in the County of New-York, he was violently assaulted and beaten by *Thomas Palmer Buckbee who jumped into deponents boat and struck him with his fist*

without any justification on the part of the said assailant: Wherefore this deponent prays that the said *Thomas*

may be bound by recognizance to be of good behaviour, and keep the peace, and to answer for the above assault, &c. at the next Court of General Sessions of the Peace to be holden in and for the said city.

Sworn before me, this *10* day of *August* 1824 {

William Slater

H Abell

Points was notorious for its street gangs, some of which were led by members of the rapidly swelling population of Irish immigrants and others by "native-born Americans." The gangs included the Dead Rabbits, the Forty Thieves (who coached up-and-coming pickpockets and murderers in their school, the Forty Little Thieves), the Roach Guards, and the Bowery Boys, an anti-Catholic and anti-immigrant gang led by "Bill the Butcher" (William Poole).

Although there were notorious episodes of crime throughout the period after the Civil War, the twentieth-century turning point for crime came in the Prohibition era, which began in 1920. The newly profitable bootlegging and rumrunning businesses brought with them huge stakes and huge risks—and a soaring murder rate. The 1932 shooting of Vincent "Mad Dog" Coll, while he was talking in a phone booth in a drugstore—a culmination of his feud with rival rumrunners Dutch Schultz and Owney "The Killer" Madden—was just one visible example. The leaders of organized crime did not go away with the end of Prohibition's "noble experiment" in 1933, but they shifted their focus to racketeering, gambling, and the narcotics trade. Coupled with the worsening economy, this made the Depression years in New York particularly dangerous, especially in poor, minority neighborhoods.

The post-Second World War changes in New York City made crime a particularly troublesome part of the dynamic of the "inner city." Decreasing employment opportunities, the exodus of the middle classes to the suburbs, declining investment in the city, and increased racial and ethnic tensions in an ever more diverse New York all contributed to making New Yorkers feel increasingly unsafe. The summer of 1977, seen as the nadir of the urban crisis, included a spectacular and notorious string of murders by David Berkowitz, who called himself the "Son of Sam," and who came to symbolize New York as the urban jungle.

Increasingly, New York crime was typically driven by drugs: heroin in the 1970s and crack in the 1980s. Multiple door locks, cans of pepper spray in purses, and "No radio" signs in cars became symbols of a sense of urban disorder. When Bernard Goetz shot four young men who confronted him on the subway in 1984, he was hailed as a hero by some New Yorkers, who felt that the only recourse left to them was to take law enforcement into their own hands. But others saw his encounter with his victims, who were African-American, as a troubling sign of the continued deterioration of race relations in New York. Race-tinged episodes, such as the assault on three black men by white teens in Howard Beach, Queens, in 1986, hit a raw nerve in a city where young black men were more likely to go to jail than to college.

In the 1990s, many of the statistics for street crime began to fall. Some credited this to the law and order regime of former federal prosecutor Mayor Rudolph Giuliani, who took on not only crime, but also visible signs of social disorder, such as litter and panhandling—most famously, the "squeegee men" who approached cars at stop lights to solicit money in exchange for an uninvited windshield wash. Others pointed to broader factors, such as a fall in the use of crack and also a decline in crime nationwide. By the first decade of the twenty-first century, New York was considered to be the safest large city in the country.

New York—where billions of dollars in stocks are traded and billions of dollars' worth of assets are managed—has also been home to some of the most spectacular cases of white-collar crime in the United States. Indeed, some of the most significant heists in New York's history were pulled off without a drop of blood. The culprits include conmen, embezzlers, real estate moguls, insider traders, and money managers. The greatest white-collar crime in American history was the one that came to light in 2008, when money manager Bernard Madoff confessed to the biggest Ponzi scheme ever known, defrauding investors of tens of billions of dollars. He was ordered to forfeit $170 billion in assets and sentenced to 150 years in prison without parole.

ARNOLD ROTHSTEIN

Among the many gangsters and racketeers who pepper the history of New York City, Arnold Rothstein ("the Brain") has a special place as the man who helped create crime organizations that were truly organized. As a bookmaker, bootlegger, and narcotics dealer, he organized his enterprises along business lines, training such successors as Meyer Lansky, Charles "Lucky" Luciano, and Dutch Schultz.

Rothstein is perhaps best remembered for having been accused of engineering the outcome of the baseball World Series of 1919 (the so-called Black Sox scandal), in which eight players from the Chicago White Sox allegedly threw the series to the Cincinnati Reds. Rothstein made a bundle on the outcome, but steadfastly denied any involvement. In 1928, he was shot and mortally wounded in a room at the Park Central Hotel at Seventh Avenue and 56th Street, possibly because of an unpaid gambling debt. His killer was never identified.

LEFT Arnold Rothstein at the New York State Supreme Court, where he was fighting a bankruptcy receiver's attempt to collect $366,000. Photograph taken on July 22, 1928.

OPPOSITE Helen Jewett was a fashionable New York prostitute who was murdered by a client in 1836; Jewett's death and Richard Robinson's trial for her murder were used by a variety of organizations and individuals to highlight the dangers of vice and unsupervised youth. The press, the *New York Herald* in particular, capitalized on the crime to publish sensational coverage of the incident.

Merchants, Workers, and Unions

New York began as a trading port, situated on one of the greatest natural harbors in the world, rich with furs, timber, and other natural resources. New Amsterdam, and later New York, became a major center of trade. The completion of the Erie Canal in 1825 accelerated the flow of staples from the country's agricultural heartland, and thousands of ships brought manufactured goods from around the world through the Port of New York, consolidating its role as the most important port in the country. It's no surprise that some of the richest and most influential families in early New York began their fortunes in the business of trading.

In the nineteenth century, New York rapidly became known for making things, as well. Beginning in the middle of the century, and stretching for more than 100 years, New York was the single biggest manufacturing city in the United States—with thousands of workshops and factories turning out everything from pianos to clothing to sugar. In the early days, these were artisan-run workshops, the names of whose master craftsmen still resonate through the ages—Myer Myers, the great silversmith, Duncan Phyfe, whose simple style helped define the American aesthetic in furniture and cabinetry, and Henry Steinway, the German immigrant who, with his brothers, moved their piano workshop from Lower Manhattan to vacant land in Queens, which they transformed into a virtual company town. (This neighborhood still bears the name of, and remains home to, the Steinway piano company.)

BELOW Women were a significant part of the labor force by 1913, when this photograph was taken. Mainly Italian and Jewish immigrants, they sewed garments by machine and by hand, and produced other fabric items such as flags. They also helped organize unions for needle-trades workers.

Factories increasingly drove the economy. By the end of the nineteenth century, some of these were massive, such as the Domino (formerly Havemeyer & Elder) sugar complex on the shore of Williamsburg, in Brooklyn, or the Pfizer pharmaceutical plant in South Williamsburg. But more often, New York's industries were decentralized, comprising countless small enterprises, like the foundries that created the cast-iron buildings for which Soho is known, or the innumerable garment shops that began in tenements and lofts and which were eventually consolidated into the Garment Center on the west side of Manhattan in the 1920s, collectively creating New York's single largest manufacturing sector.

These manufacturing industries created a huge demand for labor, and millions of workers from all over the country and the world converged in New York, seeking to take advantage of the opportunities here. Many of these new arrivals found themselves faced with harsh conditions, low wages, long hours, or discrimination, fueling New York's central role in the creation of labor unions. The city's earliest labor organizations—such as the pre-Civil War Working Men's Party and General Trades' Union—were wiped out by economic downturns in the volatile economy. However, in the years after the Civil War, as industrial manufacturing spread, New York City saw the rise not only of the Knights of Labor, which called for a union of the "productive classes" against banks and lawyers, but also of the socialist International Workingmen's Association and of the Central Labor Union, which sought to run labor candidates for office. In 1886, the union leader Samuel Gompers, an immigrant from England, became a major player in American labor history by founding the American Federation of Labor (AFL), which was committed to steering clear of politics and concentrating on organizing the skilled

LEWIS W. HINE
HASTINGS-ON-HUDSON N.Y.

workers of exclusive trades—what Gompers called "the aristocracy of labor."

But many of the workers in New York's industries did not fit into Gompers's craft union idea, and the labor movement became increasingly restless. By the late 1800s, the fortuitously named Union Square in Manhattan, at the "union" of Broadway and Fourth Avenue, had become the gathering place for countless soapbox orators, Labor Day parades, and political demonstrations. These protests were given particular urgency in the aftermath of the horrific events of March 25, 1911, when a fire broke out on the top floors of the Asch Building in the Triangle Waist Company factory, located in Greenwich Village. Although proclaimed a modern factory—a seemingly safe alternative to the thousands of dangerous sweatshops—management had locked a critical door, and thereby doomed over 100 workers, mostly young immigrant women, who lost

their lives to the fire or by jumping to their deaths. The events fueled the growth of the young International Ladies' Garment Workers' and the Amalgamated Clothing Workers of America and ushered in a new set of safety regulations.

As the twentieth century unfolded, the labor movement became an accepted player in the power structure of the city, particularly during the Depression-era administration of Mayor Fiorello La Guardia. The post-Second World War era saw major struggles over the right to organize and strike in the new public sector unions, and the municipal unions were important protagonists in the battles over the future of the city in an increasingly postindustrial era. During the turbulent 1960s and early 1970s, under the liberal administration of Mayor John V. Lindsay, New York became known as "Strike City," as transit workers, sanitation workers, police, postal workers, and others launched job actions, and the city was torn apart by a bitter and racially charged teachers' strike. Although the exodus of manufacturing jobs and the fiscal crises and policies of the late twentieth century took their toll on the influence of the labor movement in New York, the city remains today one of the centers of union influence in the country.

ABOVE Photographer Lewis Hine, known for his images documenting social conditions and working people's lives, was commissioned to document the construction of the Empire State Building in 1930. At the peak of construction, 3,500 workers were employed on the job.

HENRY GEORGE FOR MAYOR

One of the great debates of the post-Civil War labor movement was how deeply unions should get involved in politics. The closest New York came to electing a labor party candidate came in 1886, at a time when union activists concluded that the use of police and the courts against striking workers meant that they had to enter the political arena themselves. In that year, the city's Central Labor Union—a coalition of skilled and unskilled workers' organizations numbering some 50,000 members from 207 unions—founded the United Labor Party and rallied behind the mayoral campaign of Henry George, a major celebrity of the era. Seven years earlier, George had written the bestseller *Progress and Poverty*, advocating for a "single tax" on real estate to remedy class inequality in America. George campaigned on a platform calling for higher wages and shorter hours, an end to "industrial slavery," government ownership of the railroads, the end of police "intermeddling" with peaceful labor demonstrations, and the single tax. George seemed electable; indeed, he beat the young Republican candidate (and future president), Theodore Roosevelt, but lost to Democratic Abram Hewitt amidst accusations of fraud. He ran again in 1897, but died four days before the election.

LEFT London born, of Jewish parents, Samuel Gompers learned the cigar-making trade from his father. The family immigrated to New York City in 1863 and continued in the cigar-making trade there. Gompers served as president of Local 144 of the Cigar Makers' International Union (CMIU) in New York City before assuming the presidency of the labor federation he helped to establish, and he preached a strategy of "pure and simple unionism," stressing bread-and-butter issues rather than social reform or political power plays.

Wall Street

Three decades after the settlement of New Amsterdam, the Dutch West India Company built a wooden stockade at the northern boundary of their new settlement. When the British took control of the colony, they dismantled it and built a road along its former course, running from Broad Street to the East River. Wall Street, as it came to be known, quickly became a hub of the colony's commercial activity.

Wall Street was one of many locations where the city's merchants gathered to trade in stocks, bonds, and loans. The city's coffee houses, in particular, were informal meeting places where merchants, bankers, insurance sellers, and speculators came to hash out deals. But, in 1792, showing an early penchant for organization, a group of 22 merchants and brokers signed the Buttonwood Agreement, named for the buttonwood tree outside the Merchants' Coffee House at 68 Wall Street where they were meeting to conduct

business. The agreement was an attempt to smooth out the vicissitudes of the market and to standardize commission rates on the sale of securities.

After the War of 1812, a group of savvy investors decided to organize once again, this time forming the New York Stock Exchange Board, and the brokers and bankers adopted a formal constitution. The exchange quickly became home to insurance and banking stocks, and brokers would meet twice a day at the exchange to bid on stocks as they were individually called out.

In 1863, the exchange formally changed its name to the New York Stock Exchange, and two years later, it moved to its current location at the corner of Broad Street and Wall Street. By that time, the exchange was trading the first industrial securities—railroads—and over the next generation, industrialization recreated the stock exchange. By 1870, there were over 1,000 members trading at the exchange, ten times the number trading a decade earlier. On December 15, 1886, trading reached

a volume of one million shares per day. No longer a call market where auctioneers would call out each individual stock, the exchange ran a continuous auction from the opening of trading to the closing bell.

In 1901, Andrew Carnegie's US Steel became the first company listed with over one billion dollars in capitalization. America's industrial elite made their fortunes and fame through Wall Street dealings: Andrew Carnegie, Jay Gould, John D. Rockefeller, Edward Harriman, J. P. Morgan, and others emerged as titans of American finance. Their wealth was such that the nation's economy turned on their individual actions. Unscrupulous financiers such as Jay Gould attempted to corner markets, or control prices, by secretly buying available reserves and cutting backroom deals with other bankers or with government officials to limit the supply of a given commodity or security. Others became celebrities simply through high-profile deals, buying or selling major corporations, or dominating single industries. Still others used their wealth more responsibly, shoring up the market after speculative bubbles burst, as J. P.

Morgan did in 1907 when he, almost single-handedly, stabilized the markets after a run on the banks nearly bankrupted the nation's economy.

The wealth concentrated in the market fed into the American dream, and by the 1920s, Americans of all means were buying stocks with enthusiasm. But the speculation was inherently risky, and on "Black Tuesday," October 29, 1929, the market lost a quarter of its value. The crash of 1929 capped the frenzied activity of the industrial age, drawing public scrutiny along with public fascination. In 1934, Congress created the Securities and Exchange Commission to oversee the market and regulate how publicly traded companies reported to stockholders and to the public.

Following the Second World War, institutional investors replaced financial tycoons as the dominant force on Wall Street and the celebrity face faded for a generation. Employee pension funds, insurance companies, and investment banks turned to Wall Street to take advantage of the long economic boom of the postwar years, using their large pools of money to create mutual funds. Municipalities like New York City also turned to Wall Street, often to raise money for postwar social services and public works.

But, while they benefited during boom times, local governments found themselves in jeopardy during economic downturns. Stagnation in the country's economy during the 1970s, paired with the soaring costs of government, culminated in a municipal fiscal crisis in 1975. New York City came to the brink of bankruptcy when the city turned to the bond market to pay for some of its promised social services. Wall Street lost faith in the city and refused to lend it the money it needed to stay solvent. Under the leadership of Governor Hugh Carey, public officials from the State and City, along with private citizens, engineered a bailout, personally convincing the president of the teachers' union to invest $150 million of the union's pension funds in city bonds.

In more recent times, as the sub-prime mortgage crisis came to a head in the fall of 2008, Henry Paulson, Secretary of the US Treasury, and Benjamin Bernanke, the chairman of the Federal Reserve Board, went to Wall Street to meet with the heads of the nation's largest banks and to hammer out a deal to save large banks such as Goldman Sachs and Morgan Stanley. Politicians and pundits once again made "Wall Street" shorthand for complicated, even shady, investment schemes separate from the average American "Main Street." But the power of New York as a financial center endured even that assault, and the association with the old Dutch landmark remains, even as electronic trading has increasingly liberated the world of high finance from the actual confines of Wall Street.

OPPOSITE The current building of the New York Stock Exchange on Broad Street was completed in 1903. Its trading floor was a grand 109 by 140 feet, topped by an enormous skylight. The neoclassical design of the building by George B. Post was chosen from among eight competition design entries by leading New York City architects.

BELOW One of several main trading floors at the New York Stock Exchange, photographed at a relatively quiet moment in July 2010.

DOW JONES

Wealth and fame have had a long relationship in the United States. By the late nineteenth century, journalists such as Charles Dow began tracking the progress of the companies traded on the New York Stock Exchange and provided an information-hungry public with a list of celebrity financiers. Dow combined with Edward Jones to create a financial news bureau called Dow, Jones & Company. In 1883, the two were publishing the Customers' Afternoon Letter, which detailed the business of the day and included a stock index of some of the major firms traded at the exchange. By 1889, they had changed the name to the Wall Street Journal, which made the street and the exchange almost synonymous.

The index that Dow and Jones created in 1884 still bears the name the Dow Jones Industrial Average and remains the key barometer of the health of Wall Street.

Transportation in New York

The iconic image of New York transportation today may well be the yellow taxi. Getting around the city was not always as simple as hailing a cab on the street, however. New York has experimented with a wide variety of solutions for moving people throughout the city since the beginning of the nineteenth century, and the resulting—and extensive—mass transit system deserves a large measure of the credit for the city's growth, density, and ongoing success.

New York is built on an archipelago, making it in effect a city of islands. Thus the first challenge for transportation: how to cross the rivers. New Yorker Robert Fulton, inventor of the steamboat, launched the first steam ferry service between New York City and the growing bedroom communities in the City of Brooklyn, the city's first suburb, in 1814. By mid-century, 100,000 people crossed the East River daily by ferry from Brooklyn to their jobs in Manhattan. And as early as

1817, Commodore Cornelius Vanderbilt established the foundations of what would become one of the world's great fortunes by providing a freight and ferry service between Manhattan and Staten Island.

Transporting New Yorkers on land was also a challenge, to which omnibuses were an early solution. Abraham Brown revolutionized local transportation in New York when, in 1840, he established the first line of omnibuses—essentially oversized stagecoaches—creating the city's first public transport along a set route with a fixed fare. Under the company name of Kipp & Brown, his route eventually extended throughout most of Manhattan. Horse-drawn omnibuses were soon replaced by trolleys (also horse-drawn at first) and cable cars—in both cases, travel along embedded tracks made the ride smoother and faster. The construction of rail lines along Sixth and Eighth Avenues disrupted the business of the Kipp &

ABOVE The Staten Island Ferry, here photographed in February 2006, runs across New York Harbor from Staten Island to Lower Manhattan, nowadays a 25-minute trip. Ferries have made this crossing since the eighteenth century.

RIGHT The first ticket to the first segment of the Interborough Rapid Transit Company subway line was sold at Grand Central Terminal on October 27, 1904, the day the segment was completed. Note that the ticket cost a nickel and was "good for one continuous trip on any line," although only the one segment of the one line was available.

BELOW This omnibus, photographed at Madison Square, was part of a system of buses run by the Fifth Avenue Coach Company, beginning in 1885. The photograph was taken in 1900, the same year that the company ran its first "automobile stage." The last horse-drawn bus was retired in 1908.

Brown omnibus routes, eventually forcing the company to close its doors for good.

The electrification of the trolley lines in the late 1880s made them even faster, and soon the City of Brooklyn was so crisscrossed with trolley tracks (and overhead wires) that pedestrians found it difficult to cross the street (earning them the nickname "Trolley Dodgers," a moniker that would be immortalized in the name of a beloved baseball team, the Brooklyn Dodgers). The trolley lines, street railroads, and, later, the subways played a critical role in the spread of development in New York, giving rise to a series of neighborhoods throughout Brooklyn, Queens, and the Bronx, strung like beads on a chain across the formerly rural areas of the outer boroughs.

As the streets became increasingly cluttered with traffic and noise, it became highly desirable to move transit away from street level. The first important innovations in this area were the elevated railroads, the first of which were constructed in the mid-nineteenth century. Running down the avenues and casting a shadow on the streets below, these rumbling elevated trains, or "Els," were an iconic part of the Manhattan streetscape until the 1940s when, in the wake of the Depression, Mayor Fiorello La Guardia initiated their decades-long removal. In the Bronx, Brooklyn, and Queens, numerous elevated lines remain and are active to this day.

It was not until 1904 that New York, under the aegis of Chief Engineer of the New York Rapid Transit Commission, William Barclay Parsons, experienced underground transportation with the construction of the first subway line, the Interborough Rapid Transit (IRT). Parsons's IRT was soon joined by other subway companies—the Brooklyn Manhattan Transit (BMT) and

BELOW This image captures the many modes of transportation in use on Manhattan's Lower West Side as the nineteenth century came to a close—barges and ships in the harbor, horse-drawn carts and omnibuses, and above them, the elevated railroad casting shadows over the few pedestrians in evidence. The imposing structure in the right background is the Barge Office, while the small building to the left is the Press Office.

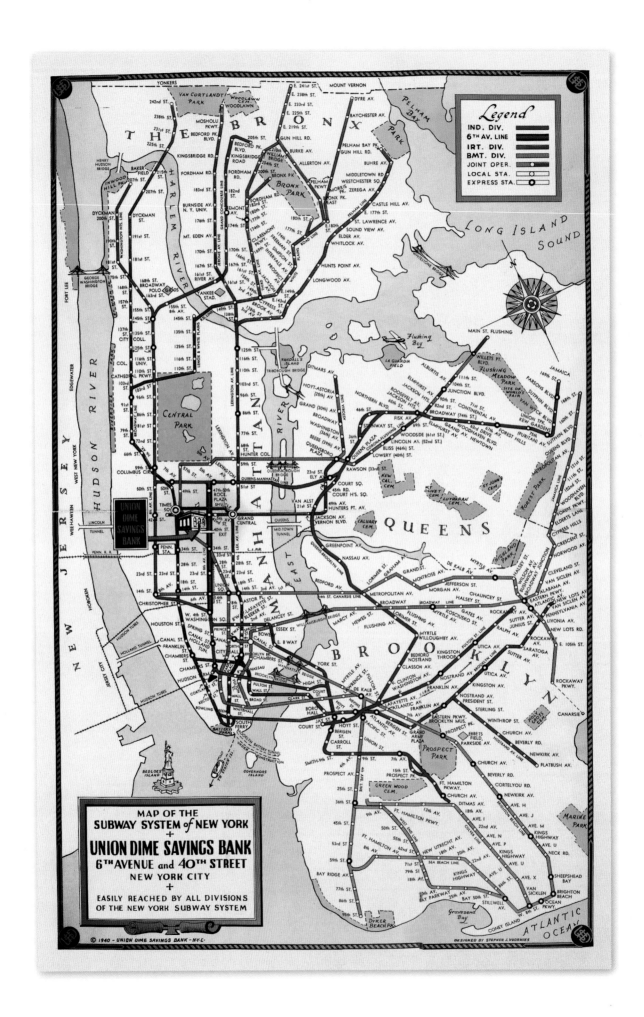

MAP OF THE
SUBWAY SYSTEM of NEW YORK
+
UNION DIME SAVINGS BANK
6TH AVENUE and 40TH STREET
NEW YORK CITY
+
EASILY REACHED BY ALL DIVISIONS
OF THE NEW YORK SUBWAY SYSTEM

© 1940 - UNION DIME SAVINGS BANK - N.Y.C.

DESIGNED BY STEPHEN J. VOORHIES

the Independent (IND)—the latter operated by the City to make the vast city easily accessible at modest cost. The legacy of the subway's diverse origins can still be seen today in the graphic markers for the various subway lines—red and green numbers for the IRT, yellow letters for the BMT, and orange letters for the IND. While the original fare of a nickel has certainly increased with the passage of time, a ride still remains a bargain. The maze of parallel and intersecting lines makes for a complex but versatile system, one in which seasoned New Yorkers learn to navigate creative routes and connections to best traverse all 722 miles.

Subways, ferries, and buses connect the five boroughs to one another, but to get into or out of the city 100 or more years ago, many travelers would have boarded trains at one of New York's main depots—Grand Central Terminal or Pennsylvania Station. The former, originally called Grand Central Depot when it opened in 1871, united three rail lines that connected the city with points north along the Hudson River, west to Buffalo, and east into Connecticut. Penn Station, named for the Pennsylvania Railroad upon its completion in 1910, allowed New Yorkers to travel south and westward by train into New Jersey and Pennsylvania. When Penn Station's pink granite walls and stately Doric pillars fell in 1963 to make room for the fourth Madison Square Garden, many New Yorkers were outraged and a movement for architectural preservation was born in the form of the Landmarks Preservation Commission.

THE SECRET SUBWAY OF 1870

By the early 1860s, downtown Manhattan's streets were clogged with traffic. The introduction of London's first subway in 1863 inspired some New Yorkers to envision a similar underground rail system. New York's businesses and landowners, however, largely opposed the idea, fearing that an excavation beneath the city's busiest streets might compromise their physical stability and decrease property values. Not to be dissuaded, the publisher, inventor, and entrepreneur Alfred Ely Beach used his own money to demonstrate the feasibility of such a project. He secretly—and illegally—built a one-block-long underground pneumatic rail line beneath Broadway between Warren and Murray Streets in 1869, under the pretense of creating pneumatic postal tubes. (He called his company the Beach Pneumatic Transit Company.) Although Beach's experimental subway enjoyed a successful trial opening in 1870, his inability to garner popular support for extended excavation soon killed it.

The Sporting Life

Most sports in nineteenth-century New York were aligned closely with gambling, in which all levels of society participated. Some activities, such as dog fighting and rat baiting—where dogs were unleashed in a small pit filled with upwards of 100–150 rats, and patrons made bets on how many the dogs could kill—were pursuits of the working class, while horse racing, boxing, rowing, and even sailing all had both working-class and elite audiences, though their experiences of the sports were vastly different.

Visitors entering the Sportsman Hall of Kit Burn (Christopher Keybourn) at 273 Water Street, in its 1850s heyday, would have been assaulted by a sensory frenzy: the din from hundreds of immigrant and working-class patrons, packed in tight quarters while cheering over snarling dogs and hissing rats; the pungent smell of beer and home-made liquor mixed with the ancient odor of the rat pit; and the strange sight of two giant stuffed dogs hanging over the bar, veterans of the hall's two prominent amusements.

The clubhouse at Jerome Park, built by the wealthy financiers Leonard Jerome and August Belmont, could not have been more different. Well-dressed denizens of New York's social elite mingled in the extensive quarters, reclining on luxurious club chairs and gilded Victorian fainting couches. Enjoying a vast estate in the wide open, rural spaces of Fordham (now the Bronx) and perched on a bluff above the course, upper-class racing fans enjoyed fresh air, expensive champagne, and expansive views of the genteel sport of harness racing.

Blood sports such as rat baiting and dog fighting

OPPOSITE On May 27, 1823, in a race that presaged the Civil War, Northern champion Eclipse defeated Southerner (Sir) Henry, the betting favorite, in a grueling best-of-three.

BELOW In the mid-nineteenth century, Hiram Woodruff was a dealer, trader, and rider of fine horses. At his stables near present-day Jerome Avenue in the Bronx, customers included such wealthy equine connoisseurs as Commodore Cornelius Vanderbilt, August Belmont, and Jay Gould.

often took place in the saloons and public houses of working-class New York neighborhoods such as Five Points, the Bowery, and along the waterfront. During the nineteenth century, these pursuits often became a target of the reformist zeal of the middle class. Henry Bergh, who founded the American Society for the Prevention of Cruelty to Animals in the 1860s, made them his special cause. By the end of that decade, rat baiting and dog fighting had been driven underground and all but eradicated.

On the other hand, boxing, another important working-class entertainment, thrived in nineteenth-century New York. Because the sport was so heavily regulated, it became tied to New York City politics, as Democratic bosses used their clout to encourage policemen to look the other way when popular fights were being held, such as when the great bare-knuckle champ John L. Sullivan defended his title in 1883. When restrictions were lifted, New York claimed the mantle of being the capital of boxing, and high-profile fights became a place for wealthy New Yorkers to see and be seen alongside working-class and middle-class fans.

Horse racing was popular among New Yorkers of every social class. Its history in the city goes back to 1665

(the year after the English took over New Amsterdam and named it New York), when colonial authorities built the Newmarket Track in what is now Hempstead, Long Island. The Church Farm Course in Lower Manhattan followed in 1725. Horse racing was banned in the early years of the Republic because of its aristocratic connotations, but resumed in 1820. Three years later, one of the most celebrated races in history took place as the nine-year-old Eclipse, representing the Northern states, beat Sir Henry, representing the South, in a best-of-three contest. A crowd of 60,000 spectators assembled at the Union Course, including Andrew Jackson and Aaron Burr. In 1845, another great North versus South match race was held, and the Southern horse Peytona defeated Fashion in front of an estimated 100,000 racegoers.

As popular as thoroughbred racing was, harness racing—or trotting—garnered even larger crowds and greater purses. Viewers could watch impromptu races down Third Avenue and Harlem Lane and, by 1825, the New York Trotting Club had brought a formal air to the races. By 1860, there were seven tracks in and around New York City. Shortly after the Civil War, thoroughbred racing returned to prominence as wealthy industrialists built elite courses such as the Jerome

ABOVE Among the water sports depicted in this hand-colored Currier & Ives lithograph, "Summer Scenes in New York Harbor," are sailing and rowing. A rowing race takes place in the foreground, the oarsmen cheered on by men in rowboats and canoes.

(Bronx, 1865), Sheepshead Bay (Brooklyn, 1885), and the Morris Park Racetrack (Bronx, 1889), while entrepreneurs selling new, cheap amusements built the enormous Brighton Beach racecourse (Brooklyn, 1879) and the Gravesend Track (Brooklyn, 1885). At the turn of the century, this expansion was rounded out with the construction of four more tracks, including the storied Aqueduct track and Belmont Park.

Even sports that are now considered to belong to the upper class, such as rowing, had working-class and popular counterparts in New York City. Men who transported people and small freight across New York City's waterways also raced each other for money, while others wagered on the races. The city's different ethnic groups often raced each other, and neighborhoods cultivated bitter rivalries. By mid-century, middle-class New Yorkers interested in tempering the effects of urban living by taking exercise were setting up rowing clubs. At the same time, students from New York's colleges began to form rowing teams, the first being Columbia in 1859. By the turn of the century, there were 31 boathouses for the city's clubs and rowing had declined in popularity among the city's immigrant population.

The history of sailing is similar. Before the Civil War, working sailors raced the small schooners and trading vessels that carried much of New York's commercial goods. Banding together in 1844, the captains of these ships formed the New York Yacht Club (NYYC) and their races were watched by thousands. Amateur sailing continued to thrive under "corinthian" sailors who sailed their own boats even after the Civil War, when the NYYC began racing larger, more expensive boats bought by wealthy owners and raced by hired professionals. In 1851, John Cox Stevens, founder of the NYYC, built *America* along with a syndicate of other sailors, and sailed in an English race sponsored by the Royal Yacht Squadron. The syndicate deeded the winning trophy to the NYYC and the club began hosting the America's Cup, which it won continuously until 1983.

RIGHT This photograph of cyclists racing on a track at Manhattan Beach was taken in 1896 by the Manhattan-based Byron Company. John Boyd Dunlop's invention of the pneumatic bicycle tire eight years earlier, in 1888, enabled higher speeds and smoother travel for bicycles and ushered in the golden age of cycling at the end of the nineteenth century, making races like this possible. While cycling has long been a favorite pastime of New Yorkers, it has evolved from a leisure activity and spectator sport into an efficient and environmentally friendly form of urban transportation, with more than 620 miles of bicycle lanes in New York City today.

SIX-DAY RACES

Bicycling first became a craze in New York in the 1860s, when velocipedes began making an appearance in the still-new Central Park. But the 1890s, with the introduction of the safety bike, heralded the true "bicycle era" in the city. New York soon became famous in the cycling world for the legendary six-day races (both men's and women's) that were inaugurated at the original Madison Square Garden, designed by Stanford White, on Madison Avenue at 26th Street. The races, the team version of which became known as "Madisons," were set to test who could do the most laps over a six-day period. As event competition grew, riders increasingly pushed their limits, some attempting to ride for over 24 hours without sleeping. Rumors of drug use, exhaustion, hallucinations, and bodily injuries make these six-day races one of the first examples of an extreme entertainment sport.

Pleasure Grounds

Appreciating public space has not always been second nature to New Yorkers. Although Bowling Green, the first official park in New York City, was established in 1733 "for the Beauty and Ornament ... as well as for the Recreation & Delight of the Inhabitants of this City," most early solutions to remedy the cramped conditions of the metropolis and meet the desire for recreational facilities often designated waterfronts, vacant lots, or even cemeteries—notably Green-Wood Cemetery in the City of Brooklyn—as valuable open spaces for recreation and socializing rather than the establishment of formal parks. It was not until the yellow fever and cholera epidemics of 1798, 1822, 1832, and 1845 that the rise of the gymnastic and exercise movement prompted the city to develop more official recreational areas, which by the twentieth century would eventually include ballparks, playgrounds, ball and racket courts, and swimming pools among many other facilities.

The original street plan of Manhattan, laid out in 1811, anticipated a series of public squares scattered through the grid, but no large parks. However, the plan was modified over time. The year 1847 saw the opening of both Madison Square Park and Reservoir Square, which was renamed Bryant Park in 1884 after the *New York Evening Post* editor William Cullen Bryant. Bryant was also an advocate for the construction of what would become one of New York City's most recognizable physical features, Central Park, and used editorial space in his paper to lobby for its creation. In 1853, in a visionary move, the City's Common Council appropriated funds to purchase a large area of land for the creation of a park and the idea of Central Park began to take shape.

The site proposed was Jones Wood, 150 acres on the East Side between 66th and 75th Street; but the site that was eventually chosen, after a great debate, ran for 2½ miles up the center of the island, and required displacing some 1,600 people—mostly poor immigrants and African-Americans—from their homes. Of the 33 competing entries proposing a plan for the construction of Central Park, the one drawn up by Frederick Law

LEFT Stansbury Norse's 1888 painting depicts the blockhouse in Central Park, a fort built in 1814 as defense against the British. It stands today as the oldest remaining structure in Central Park, at 109th Street and Central Park West, a section that was incorporated into the park in 1863.

ABOVE Johann Mongles Culverhouse depicted skaters on the pond in Central Park in 1865. Skating was a favorite activity in the mid-nineteenth century; Central Park's first organized skating area started in 1858 before the park itself was even officially opened. On busy days, tens of thousands of people were reported to skate on the lake.

Olmsted and Calvert Vaux was selected in 1858. Olmsted was named Architect-in-Chief of the project and Vaux was retained as Consulting Architect. Later that same year, the lower areas of the park opened to the public—it was the first landscaped park in the United States and to this day an icon of life in New York. It was soon followed by Prospect Park in Brooklyn, also designed by Olmsted and Vaux.

With the early twentieth century—the so-called "Progressive Era"—came a surge in support for recreational areas, and particularly for playgrounds

and drinking fountains. Such advocates as Theodore Roosevelt championed recreational facilities as an essential part of making the city's citizens "contented and law-abiding," while advocates of public drinking fountains, pioneered in particular by supporters of the Temperance Movement, claimed that access to potable water provided alternatives to saloons and alcohol consumption. However, many early recreational facilities encouraged alcohol consumption and other pleasure activities. The Elysian Fields of Hoboken were an early "amusement park" complete with liquor,

cigars, rides, gambling, ball fields, rustic walks, etc. Coney Island in Brooklyn began to attract vacationers in the mid-1800s due to its close proximity to the metropolis. By the early decades of the twentieth century, its three amusement parks—Steeplechase Park, Luna Park, and Dreamland—were catering to the appetites of the urban masses, providing a fantasy land that allowed people to escape the realities of the dense city and let loose.

The city's single greatest era of park-building began under Robert Moses in 1938. As the first citywide Commissioner of Parks, Moses more than doubled the city's parkland from 14,000 to 34,673 acres and increased its number of playgrounds from 119 to 779 in his 26 years in the position. Whereas Olmsted and Vaux designed naturalistic landscapes for relaxation, Moses built athletic fields and playgrounds for active play, including creating Flushing Meadows Corona Park in Queens, Randall's Island Park and Wards Island Park in the East River, and Jones Beach on Long Island, and significantly renovating Central Park. One of the most controversial figures in New York history, Moses was

vilified by many for the impact of his road-building on residential neighborhoods and his top-down approach to planning, but his record on park-building earned him praise even from many of his critics.

In recent years, many abandoned or neglected city spaces have been reclaimed by "grassroots" activists intent on bringing green space to New York residents, and these open spaces have in turn been reinstituted as official facilities maintained by the city. The High Line, an aerial greenway, is one such park opened to the public in 2009, which runs along the lower west side of Manhattan. It was built on a section of the abandoned elevated freight railroad spur called the West Side Line, which was last operated in the 1980s. The reclaiming of such spaces has additional economic and social benefits for the communities surrounding them, attracting developers who have created amusements such as restaurants, shops, and cultural facilities. Today, the city continues to rethink abandoned and neglected spaces in creative ways, paving the way for a new generation of open spaces.

ABOVE Samuel Gottscho, later known as an architectural photographer, was an accomplished amateur in 1906 when he captured Luna Park, Coney Island. Along with Steeplechase Park and Dreamland, it was a fantastical escape for New York's working and middle classes at the turn of the century.

RIGHT Taken in August 2009, this view of the new High Line—a disused elevated railway line converted into a park and footpath route—shows the first part of the line to be completed, from Gansevoort Street to 20th Street.

BELOW A vintage postcard from the 1950s showing a bird's eye view looking north toward Central Park and upper Manhattan atop the 70 storey RCA Building.

AGITATING FOR CENTRAL PARK

The press was one of the more effective avenues for garnering support for recreational areas and parks during the 1850s. Advocates of open public spaces, such as the poet William Cullen Bryant, editor of the *Evening Post*, and Horace Greeley, editor of the *Tribune*, published numerous letters and editorials outlining the benefits of fresh air and water for city dwellers. Landscape gardener Andrew Jackson Downing wrote extensively on the subject, praising London's parks and stressing their elevating effects on the population. These advocates held the common vision that public spaces had the potential not only to alleviate the tensions of congested living conditions in the growing metropolis, but also to advance rapport among various social classes. Their editorials raised the park question to the status of political issue, so when Ambrose C. Kingsland was elected to the office of mayor in 1851, after having included the issue in his political campaign, he advanced a plan to purchase a large area of land for a central park. The Common Council approved the selected site and the proposal submitted by landscape architect Frederick Law Olmsted and architect Calvert Vaux won the commission for the great park's design.

LEFT Aerial view of Central Park, Manhattan, looking south. Photographed on July 1, 2006, this picture clearly shows the park's vital role as a lung for the intense urban area, as well as for outdoor activities.

On Broadway

I n one sense, Broadway is just one street cutting through the length of Manhattan. But it is also "The Great White Way," synonymous with the commercial center of American theater. It was along this avenue that the American vaudeville tradition was first advertised and that musical theater was born. Culminating in a theater district that encompasses nearly 30 city blocks, the electric flash and energy of twenty-first-century Broadway theaters can be traced back to a popular tradition that began in New York before the American Revolution.

Like the City of New York and Broadway itself, New York theater had its origins at the southernmost tip of Manhattan. The first playhouses in New York appeared in the 1730s at the base of Broadway Street. The Park Theatre (originally known as the New Theatre)—the first New York theater built after Independence—stood at the corner of Park Row and Broadway. Opened in 1798, for nearly a decade it was the only dedicated playhouse in Manhattan. Gradually, other theaters began to spring up along Broadway and the nearby Bowery. Popular entertainments such as variety, burlesque, and minstrel shows amused the working-class denizens of the Bowery while the playhouses on Broadway performed more refined dramatic productions and operas. The two routes converged at Union Square, which by the late 1800s was New York's theater district.

It was in Union Square that Tony Pastor established a new genre of variety entertainment. At the time that he opened his new theater in 1881, in the same building that housed Tammany Hall, variety shows had a reputation for crude songs and vulgar comic situations, and they were being performed for crowds of rowdy men. Seeking to appeal to women and children, Pastor ran his variety shows throughout the day and featured more genteel and child-friendly entertainments such as magicians, acrobats, and trained animals. He even instituted rules for audience conduct. In an effort to distance his entertainments from variety shows, Pastor christened his acts "vaudeville."

Vaudeville was not the only form of entertainment to originate in New York. In 1866, a theater at 537 Broadway, Niblo's Garden, saw the birth of the American musical. Originally conceived as a standard melodrama, *The Black Crook* became arguably the first musical when producers sought to salvage their investment in a French ballet troupe that lacked a performance space. In incorporating the dance troupe, *The Black Crook* became an extravagant spectacle that united drama, dance, music, and flamboyant costumes.

The show was wildly popular, grossing over one million dollars.

Musical theater came together as a blend of performance traditions. The operettas and songs of the Yiddish stage in New York's Lower East Side were attended by a young Irving Berlin. The bang and crash sounds from Tin Pan Alley (28th Street between Broadway and Sixth Avenue) attracted the youthful energies of George M. Cohan, Cole Porter, and George and Ira Gershwin. These talents got swept uptown to the stages of Herald Square, and later, Times Square.

The form of musical theater has evolved throughout the twentieth century. *Showboat*, the first "musical play," opened in 1927 at the Ziegfeld Theatre near Times Square. With book and lyrics by Oscar Hammerstein II and Jerome Kern, the show took on controversial racial issues and incorporated original musical numbers and dialogue to form an artistically cohesive whole. In 1943, Hammerstein enhanced the form when his first collaboration with composer Richard Rodgers produced *Oklahoma!*, which is considered to be the first "book musical," fully integrating emotionally evocative song and dance numbers into the action of a plot. The book musical found a wide range of creative expression with composers and lyricists such as Frank Loesser, and the teams of Betty Comden and Adolph Green, and Frederick Loewe and Alan Jay Lerner. Productions such as *Guys and Dolls*, *West Side Story*, and *Hair* presented contemporary stories against the changing backdrop of New York City. And, as the twentieth century wore on, the form was expanded by the work of Stephen Sondheim and Andrew Lloyd Webber. Today, new talent continues to inform musical theater—through the work of such artists as Jonathan Larson, Julie Taymor, and Lin-Manuel Miranda—with different theatrical traditions and popular music styles being absorbed.

Since *Oklahoma!*, musical theater has dominated the Broadway playhouses. While straight plays can have successful runs, 27 of the 30 longest-running productions on Broadway are musicals. But—especially during the 1940s and 1950s—changing lifestyles and attitudes were the source of a more adventurous type of theater than was generally presented on the Broadway stage, which was driven by the box office. The goal of companies such as the Living Theater (founded 1947) and Circle in the Square (founded 1951) was to challenge audiences in smaller, more intimate spaces. In fact, the term "Off-Broadway" was first associated with these experimental companies, but as performance spaces gave way to more commercial fare, the definitions of Broadway and Off-Broadway changed. Today, "Broadway" refers to theaters that seat at least 500 people, "Off-Broadway" spaces range from 99–499 seats, and "Off-Off Broadway" refers to performance venues with fewer than 99 seats. It is in Off-Off Broadway productions that the experimental performance tradition most strongly continues.

Off-Off Broadway and Off-Broadway theaters are located throughout the boroughs of New York City, but the home of the Broadway stage has been Times Square for the last century. Broadway today is made up of 40 theaters, 33 of which were built before 1930. According to the Broadway League, the national trade association for the Broadway theater industry, attendance for the 2009–2010 season totaled nearly 12 million. The season opened 39 new productions and reached a record gross of over one billion dollars. "The Great White Way" is over 100 years old and counting.

PREVIOUS PAGE, LEFT The Automatic Vaudeville Theater, at 48 East 14th Street, offered a variety of entertainments, including peep shows, phonographs, a shooting gallery, and early moving pictures in the opening years of the twentieth century. It was founded in 1903 by Adolph Zukor, who went on to be one of the founders of Paramount Pictures.

PREVIOUS PAGE, RIGHT Ethel Barrymore as Madame Trentoni in Clyde Fitch's play *Captain Jinks of the Horse Marines*, ca.1901. Ethel was a member of the famous Barrymore family of New York actors, which also included her father Maurice Barrymore, her uncle John Drew, Jr., her brothers John and Lionel Barrymore, and, later, her nephew John Drew Barrymore and great-niece Drew Barrymore.

RIGHT Thomas D. Rice, an itinerant performer whose trademark offering was "Jump, Jim Crow," was a hit at the American Theater on the Bowery in 1833. According to legend, Rice based his routine on the dance of an elderly black stable hand. Wearing blackface (burnt-cork makeup), he set a fashion for white-performers-only minstrel shows that lasted until the mid-1850s.

THE STRUGGLE FOR BROADWAY

As the theatrical scene in New York grew, competing production companies fought to dominate Broadway. In 1896, a group of New York producers, including Charles Frohman, Marc Klaw, and Abe Erlanger, Jr., formed a loose partnership. The resulting "Syndicate" came to dominate not only the Broadway stage, but also touring productions that spread theater made in New York to the rest of the county. If a production chose to perform at an independent theater, it was banned from ever performing in a Syndicate playhouse. As the Syndicate owned the majority of theaters along all the major railroad routes, this made it financially impossible to avoid partnering with them. The organization took profits away from local managers and drove many out of business.

In 1907, three brothers challenged the dominance of the Syndicate and built the business behind many of Broadway's greatest hits. Lee, Sam, and J.J. Shubert established a centrally managed corporation, and purchased, built, and assembled a network of theaters throughout the country that broke the Syndicate's monopoly. The United States government later ruled the Shuberts a monopoly in turn, and in the 1950s forced them to sell 12 theaters and abandon their booking business. Today, the Shubert Organization owns 17 theaters in New York as well as the ticket service Telecharge.

LEFT Times Square at Broadway in New York City, photographed in March 2010. The vibrant heart of the city's theater district, a role it has filled for around 100 years, continues to pulse with neon and excitement.

Land of the Skyscraper

For an average city, a population increase simply means having to construct more buildings within its limits or, in the case of a city such as Los Angeles, expanding those limits through "urban sprawl." New York, however, enjoys no such luxury—particularly on the island of Manhattan. With rivers at its edges and its streets densely filled, there is, as a rule, no place to build but upward. "This [fact]," writes E. B. White in *Here Is New York*, "is responsible for [the city's] physical majesty."

At the beginning of the twentieth century, New York was a focal point for the French Beaux-Arts architectural movement. The most remarkable work to emerge from this tradition is probably the Flatiron Building, designed by Daniel Burnham and completed in 1902, whose limestone and terracotta frontage and unusual triangular shape have secured it a place in Manhattan's architectural pantheon. Standing at 285 feet, it was also one of the tallest buildings in the city, with the help of its steel-skeleton frame.

As construction and engineering technologies advanced, though, New York was consistently in the lead in constructing the world's tallest buildings. (Indeed, New York architects and developers were in a race only with themselves, with all twelve of the "world's tallest buildings" up until 1974 being constructed here.) From 1890 to the early 1930s, of the structures that ranked as the world's tallest building, all but one was in New York City. Sixteen of the city's 82 tallest buildings were constructed here, some of which have become New York's most iconic landmarks. In 1908, the Singer Building, designed by Ernest Flagg, achieved 612 feet, making it the tallest building in the world; within a few years, the Woolworth Building had gained that title. British poet Rupert Brooke wrote of the two buildings: "Their strength, almost severity, of line and the lightness of their colour gave a kind of classical feeling, classical, and yet not of Europe. It had the air, this block of masonry, of edifices built to satisfy some faith ... It came upon me, at that moment, that they could not have been dreamed and made without some nobility."

Probably the most important moment in the history of New York City architecture was the development of the Art Deco skyscraper, whose bold geometric forms and patterns expressed the eclectic art and design style that first flourished in Paris in the 1920s. In 1930, the Chrysler Building, a classic example of the style, which still ranks among New York's finest buildings, became the new tallest building in the world at 1,047 feet. It held that honor for only 18 months, however;

OPPOSITE Berenice Abbott took this photograph, titled "City Arabesque," in 1938 from the balcony of the observation room atop the Cities Service Building at Pine Street and Wall Street, then the tallest building in Lower Manhattan. The view looks northwest through the iron Art Deco railing.

RIGHT The Flatiron Building, at 175 Fifth Avenue, where it intersects with Broadway, seen from the platform of the Empire State Building. Designed primarily by Chicago architect Daniel Burnham, the 22-story, 285-foot-high triangular Flatiron was completed in 1902.

in 1931, it was superseded in height by the Empire State Building. Also designed in the Art Deco style by the firm of Shreve, Lamb & Harmon, the Empire State Building was conceived during the economic boom of the 1920s and had the misfortune to open during the Great Depression. The building was erected at the record-breaking pace of four and a half floors per week. This bold act encompassed the steadfast spirit for which New York is known. The Empire State Building became the tallest building in the world, its basic structure outstripping the Chrysler Building by a mere two feet. To prevent the building from being overtaken by an even taller structure in the near future, developer John J. Raskob arranged for a dirigible-mooring mast to be built atop the 86th floor, adding an extra 200 feet and making the building 102 stories and 1,250 feet high.

New York's next architectural design foray was the adoption of the modernist International Style, in which simple, box-like volumes were clad in curtain walls of metal and glass according to the design principles of the German architect Ludwig Mies van der Rohe. The first major International Style building to be constructed in New York was the United Nations Secretariat Building in the UN complex, built on spacious grounds overlooking the East River, which had been donated by John D. Rockefeller, Jr. in the Turtle Bay neighborhood of Manhattan. Lever House, 390 Park Avenue at East 53rd Street, designed by Gordon Bunshaft of Skidmore, Owings & Merrill, is another preeminent example of the International Style. It was built in 1951–52 as the headquarters of the soap company Lever Brothers.

The early 1970s saw the expansion of Modernism in New York's skyline. The twin towers of the World Trade Center, completed in 1972, exemplified Modernism's stark rejection of ornamentation and use of new materials. With its towers' heights of 1,368 and 1,362 feet (110 stories), the World Trade became the world's tallest building, but it had many detractors among architectural critics, not to mention the general public. Designed by the Japanese architect Minoru Yamasaki, who used a tube-framed structural design with facades sheathed in aluminum alloy, the towers and other buildings like them were described by critic Lewis Mumford as "glass-and-metal filing cabinets" and as an "example of the purposeless giantism and technological exhibitionism that are now eviscerating the living tissue of every great city." Today the Twin Towers are remembered for the tragic destruction of the World Trade Center on September 11, 2001, at the hands of terrorists. But even this brutal blow could not snuff out the city's upward spirit, for plans are—at the time of writing—underway to construct a new World Trade Center, which will include a skyscraper, larger than the original two, to rival the world's tallest.

Postmodernism truly entered the New York architectural picture in the early 1980s, with Philip Johnson's historicist AT&T Building and other attempts to return to traditional styles. Today, designers of New York skyscrapers embrace both the modern—Neil Denari's angular condominium on the High Line, for example—and the romantic, best exemplified by Robert A. M. Stern's limestone-clad 15 Central Park West. Their buildings join others by contemporary "starchitects" that are transforming the city's skyline.

OPPOSITE Famed architectural renderer Hughson Hawley depicted the planned Woolworth Building in this 1910 watercolor. He emphasized the verticality of Cass Gilbert's design, soaring over the buildings of Lower Manhattan, including the steeple of Trinity Church on the horizon at the lower left.

BELOW Samuel Gottscho photographed the United Nations in 1956, soon after it opened in its new home in Manhattan. In the foreground is the General Assembly Building; behind it is the imposing 39-story Secretariat Building.

THE EMPIRE STATE BUILDING

When the Empire State Building, then the world's tallest skyscraper, opened in 1931 on the first of May—the traditional start date for New York City's commercial leases—it had an occupancy rate of about 23 percent. The Great Depression notwithstanding, a new building with a 50 percent occupancy rate was considered to be off to a slow start. Rentals were so slow, in fact, that by November 1931 the building was being called the Empty State Building. By 1935, management was turning the lights on in empty offices in an attempt to persuade potential tenants that the building was nearly full. But as the city emerged from the depths of the Depression, the Empire State Building was eventually fully rented. It remains a prime business location in addition to being one of the city's most frequently visited tourist sites.

OPPOSITE Manhattan's Chrysler Building, located at 42nd Street and Lexington Avenue, and seen here with the Empire State Building behind it, was completed in 1930 and is still the world's tallest steel-supported brick building. The Empire State Building, completed in 1931, stands at Fifth Avenue and West 34th Street.

LEFT This Wurts Brothers skyline photograph from 1939 shows how the Empire State Building looked before the antenna was added to the building's spire in 1953. The spire was originally designed as a mooring mast for dirigibles.

The Five-Borough City

For most of its history, the City of New York was located only on Manhattan: it began with the settlement of New Amsterdam at its southern tip and gradually expanded northward. Over time, another city developed across the East River—Brooklyn—and a collection of towns and villages dotted the landscapes of Staten Island (across Upper New York Bay from Manhattan), the section of Long Island north and east of Brooklyn (present-day Queens), and the area of the North American mainland closest to Manhattan (now the Bronx).

Plans to unite the municipalities around New York Harbor had been presented throughout the nineteenth century. In 1856, State Senator Cyrus P. Smith actually called for the joining together of Manhattan and Brooklyn, filling in the East River with gravel! After the end of the Civil War in 1865, the New York region enjoyed an economic boom that gave impetus to the idea of a greater New York. In 1868, Andrew Haswell Green, then a member of the Central Park Commission, proposed the consolidation of the city with the population centers that surrounded it.

Green, a successful lawyer, businessman, and political operative, argued that the "multiplicity of conflicting authorities" stymied large-scale development and prevented the region's inhabitants from recognizing their common interests. Green could not get support from the New York State Legislature, which had jurisdiction over such things, and the only progression toward the realization of his dream came in 1874, when the City of New York annexed a portion of Westchester County (now the South Bronx).

The opening of the East River (Brooklyn) Bridge in 1883, linking Manhattan and Brooklyn, revived talk of consolidation, and by 1888 both the Chamber of Commerce of the State of New York and the influential trade publications *Real Estate Record* and *Builders' Guide* were advocating the consolidation of the area around New York Harbor to improve the region's economy. Supporters of consolidation believed that the new metropolis would become one of the world's great cities—a shining symbol of America's new role as a predominant international economic power. Abram S. Hewitt, mayor of New York from 1887–88, spoke of

New York's "imperial destiny as the greatest city in the world."

In 1890, the New York State Legislature passed an act to "create a commission to inquire into the expediency of consolidating the various municipalities in the State of New York occupying the several islands in the harbor of New York." Green served as president of this commission, which included prominent businessmen from the entire region, City Parks Department landscape architect Calvert Vaux, and a state engineer. The Consolidation Bill that the commission introduced in the state legislature in 1892, however, died without coming to a vote. Two years later, voters throughout the affected region approved a nonbinding referendum calling for consolidation. In the meantime, both the City of New York and the City of Brooklyn took steps to annex additional territory. Manhattan added the remainder of the region later known as the Bronx. Brooklyn's annexation of the towns of Flatbush, Gravesend, and New Utrecht made it the third largest city in the nation.

Finally, in 1896, the New York State Legislature approved the Consolidation Bill over the objections

of both Mayor William Strong of New York City and Mayor Frederick W. Wurster of Brooklyn. The Charter of Greater New York, drafted by a state commission appointed in 1896, was signed into law on May 4, 1897, and Greater New York became an official entity on January 1, 1898. Greater New York comprised five administrative divisions called boroughs, each coexistent with one county: Manhattan (New York County), Brooklyn (Kings County), Queens (Queens County), Staten Island (Richmond County), and the Bronx (Bronx County).

Brooklyn, in particular, resisted being swallowed up by the larger political entity. Some upper-class Brooklynites feared that an influx of working-class immigrants from Manhattan would destroy the character of their city. Many other residents of the City of Brooklyn worried that the unique qualities and interests of the borough would be lost within Greater New York. Anti-consolidation campaign literature was filled with images of a large monster (Greater New York) devouring valiant Brooklyn. On New Year's Eve, 1897, Brooklyn leaders held a solemn observance of the "passing" of the City of Brooklyn. At this observance, the editor of the *Brooklyn Eagle*, St. Clair McKelway, exhorted listeners to retain their independence in the new metropolis "by loyal adherence to Brooklyn interests, to Brooklyn names, and to Brooklyn ideas … Let us be no branch office."

At its creation, Greater New York was the world's largest city apart from London, encompassing a total of 327 square miles (35 miles at its greatest length and 18¼ miles at its greatest width). According to *King's Bird's-Eye View of Greater New York* (1905), the metropolis had about 1,800 miles of paved streets (plus about 1,100 miles of unpaved streets), 1,200 miles of railroads (single track, including elevated), and 1,600 miles of sewers. Its population of nearly four million required 460 million gallons of water every day. The enthusiasm for quantification evident in the book, and in the writings of journalists of the period in general, overshadowed a far more important story: the diversity of the communities and individuals with varying—and often conflicting—perspectives, which the formation of Greater New York brought together. Those differences have fueled the unique and dynamic history of New York City over the past century and longer.

ABOVE Everyday Brooklyn life on Front Street, between Main Street and Fulton Street, in 1817–20. The thriving community shows diverse occupations and inhabitants, including African Americans, who in 1820 represented about 15 percent of the city's population. The painting is a copy by Louisa Ann Coleman of a work by Francis Guy.

EARLY BROOKLYN

Before the nineteenth century, Brooklyn was a farming town whose chief market was Manhattan, across the East River via ferry. After the introduction of the steam ferry in 1814, Brooklyn developed into one of the world's first commuter suburbs. It was known for its quiet streets, and its abundance of houses of worship led to the nickname "City of Churches." By the time of consolidation, it was a full-fledged city, with its own Brooklyn *Daily Eagle*, a baseball team (the Brooklyn Dodgers), art museum (the Brooklyn Museum), library system, and park (Prospect Park) designed by Frederick Law Olmsted and Calvert Vaux, who had earlier designed Manhattan's Central Park. Today, it is the most populous of New York's five boroughs, with over 2.5 million people; if it were still an independent city, it would be one of the largest in the nation.

LEFT The building of the Brooklyn Bridge was a key moment in the linking of what were then two cities—New York and Brooklyn. The suspension construction of the Bridge is revealed clearly in this 1881 photograph. With its use of twisted-steel cable, an innovation of the engineer John Augustus Roebling (the cables measure 15 ¾" in diameter), the bridge was the first suspension bridge of its type and the first span bridge of such prodigious length; its construction inaugurated the era of modern bridge building. US suspension bridges built after it, including the Manhattan and George Washington bridges in New York and the Golden Gate Bridge in San Francisco, derived much of their engineering methods from this project.

Bohemia

New York has witnessed two incarnations of Bohemia. First, there was the Bohemia of the Czech immigrants to New York City, who were called "Bohemians" after the medieval kingdom that became part of the Austrian empire. The Czechs came in substantial numbers in the middle of the nineteenth century and first settled on Manhattan's Lower East Side (Avenue B became known as Czech Boulevard), working primarily as cigar makers. As their numbers increased, they spread to Manhattan's Upper East Side, building a Bohemian National Hall on East 73rd Street in 1910, and venturing out to Queens, where Bohemian Hall, constructed in the neighborhood of Astoria in the same year, was later augmented by a beer garden and is today the last of New York City's large beer gardens.

And then there was the "Bohemia" that harbored romantic alternatives to mainstream society. In Manhattan, this took root in the downtown neighborhood of Greenwich Village, which was appropriated by culturally adventurous New Yorkers during the first quarter of the twentieth century. The Village, its proud colonial history and nineteenth-century reputation as a high-class quarter notwithstanding, was in a dilapidated state at the time, many of its "first families" having escaped to less tawdry environs uptown, and its formerly stately homes converted into inexpensive rooming houses. The availability of cheap housing attracted immigrants and artists, and the resultant colorful multicultural atmosphere was a nurturing ground for creative expression.

The bohemians of Greenwich Village were far outnumbered by working-class families, new ethnic groups, and patrician class holdovers from the nineteenth century, but they nevertheless acquired fame for their community as an incubator of protest—America's "Left Bank." Activities that would have been frowned upon in other parts of the city were accepted there. Gay men and lesbians could live free from societal fetters; black artists and writers from Harlem were welcome in the progressive political and social scene; suffragists demonstrated in Washington Mews; feminism, psychoanalysis, and Bolshevism were in vogue. In fact, the Village celebrated all kinds of eccentricities.

The neighborhood in Greenwich Village that became known as America's "Latin Quarter" fostered the debut of the Provincetown Players, whose innovative New York productions were first staged in 1916 in a MacDougal Street brownstone one door away from the anarchist-run Polly's Restaurant. Over on Washington Square South, beginning in 1914, Bruno's Garret drew crowds to its offbeat performances, whose focus on local issues and nontraditional staging challenged the conventional

OPPOSITE The Bohemian National Hall, shown here in 1905, was built in 1896 in a grand Renaissance Revival style, as a social, cultural, and community center for the city's Czech and Slovak population.

RIGHT New York City's "Stonewall 25" Gay Pride march, marking the movement's 25th anniversary (it is considered to have begun on the day of the Stonewall Rebellion) on June 26, 1994. Marchers are carrying a mile-long rainbow banner up First Avenue to Central Park.

forms of Broadway theater. Freethinkers flocked to the Liberal Club to hear lectures on such topics as Cubism and eugenics, and Village feminists rallied at Heterodoxy, a local luncheon club for "unorthodox women; women who did things and did them openly." *The Masses*, *Seven Arts*, and the *Little Review*, among other provocative "little magazines" headquartered in the Village, created a forum for new writers. A significant number of the artists participating in the groundbreaking "First International Exhibition of Modern Art in America," also known as the "Armory Show" of 1913, were Village residents.

The most expressive event of the period was the "Arch Rebellion" of 1917, when six conspirators, including the artists John Sloan and Marcel Duchamp, broke into a stairwell leading to the top of the Washington Square Arch and, on reaching its summit, released balloons, fired cap guns, and announced that Greenwich Village was seceding from the Union and would henceforth be known as the "Free and Independent Republic of Washington Square."

Around the time of US entry into the First World War, the Village began to commercialize, as local entrepreneurs catered to curious outsiders with tours and atmospheric eateries. The popular peddling of the unorthodox rites and behavior of the Village diluted their eccentric glamour and belied the true bohemian culture's contempt for bourgeois values. In the 1920s, the vibrant counterculture also dissipated as local civic organizations began a campaign to rehabilitate the neighborhood's tumbledown housing, and real estate interests started new developments. The Great Depression of the 1930s stymied those efforts, but the creative types had already relocated, disgusted with the high rents and with the district's loss of character.

After the Second World War, the dynamic bohemianism of the Village resurfaced as a new wave of artists moved in. The Beat Generation arrived and with it radical social and artistic experimentation. Avant-garde writers such as Allen Ginsberg and Amiri Baraka, and Abstract Expressionist painters such as Jackson Pollock and Franz Kline, became the vanguard voices of the day. In the 1950s and 1960s, Greenwich Village was the cradle of the folk music revival, which saw two unknowns named Joan Baez and Bob Dylan strumming their guitars on street corners and in tiny cafes. Storefront theaters on Bleecker Street presented unorthodox fare, which was championed by the newspaper *Village Voice*, first published in 1955.

A large gay community developed along Christopher Street. Largely tolerated by local residents, this community

BELOW Jessie Tarbox Beals is widely considered to be the world's first female photojournalist. This image, ca.1918, is from her series on Greenwich Village's Bohemian culture; it shows sculptor Edith Unger, the owner of the Mad Hatter Tea Room on West 4th Street. The Tea Room's slogan, "Down the Rabbit Hole," is in mirror writing on the lower right; on the wall is an inscription taken from Lewis Carroll's *Alice's Adventures in Wonderland*: "We're all mad here–I'm mad, you're mad. You must be, or you wouldn't have come here."

faced considerable police prejudice and violence. A confrontation in June 1969 between police and patrons of the Stonewall Inn, a gay bar on Christopher Street, led to the riot known as the Stonewall Rebellion and is regarded as the catalyst for the modern gay rights movement.

As the 1970s began, the Village saw anti-Vietnam War protests, increased gay activism, and psychedelic drug experimentation, among other nontraditional pursuits. Tourists continued to flock to the Village as a cradle of colorful nonconformity and do so still, even though the district's multimillion-dollar apartments and high-end boutiques are out of the reach of most of the artists, writers, and revolutionaries who once lived there and gave the neighborhood its storied past.

FOLK MUSIC REVIVAL

Greenwich Village was a center for folk music in the 1930s, the form serving as an important vehicle for political expression and a rallying sound for labor and other forms of protest during the Great Depression. Pete Seeger, one of the best-known folk singers of that era, went on to help revive the folk music scene in the 1950s and 1960s as the soundtrack for the Civil Rights and anti-Vietnam War movements. Midwesterner Bob Dylan was lured to the Village to perform his songs, and clubs such as Gerdes Folk City, on West 4th Street and Mercer Street, helped to launch other influential voices, among them Joan Baez and Peter, Paul, and Mary.

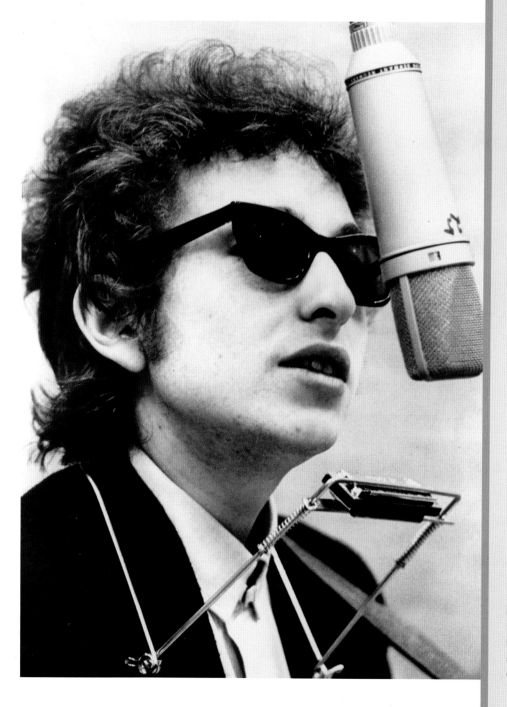

LEFT Bob Dylan recording his album *Bringing It All Back Home* in January 1965 at Columbia's Studio A in New York City, a harmonica around his neck. Dylan's mournful, contemplative songs were emblematic of the times, and of the ambience of Greenwich Village.

LEFT Washington Square is the symbolic heart of Greenwich Village, the capital of Bohemian New York. In this panoramic view by Berenice Abbott, taken in 1936, the Washington Arch is in the center. The large building behind it, and to the right, is One Fifth Avenue, a 29-story Art Deco apartment building at the southeast corner of Fifth Avenue and 8th Street (1929). Visible in the middle distance is the Empire State Building at Fifth Avenue and 34th Street.

97

Harlem and Spanish Harlem

The geographic boundaries of the northern Manhattan neighborhood known as Harlem have shifted over time, largely as a result of changes in the ethnic composition of its population, but today they generally encompass, on the west side of Manhattan, 110th Street to 155th Street, and on the east side of Manhattan, 96th Street to 142nd Street. Celebrated in story and song as cultural capitals for Americans of African-American and Latin American descent, respectively, the two neighborhoods have hosted a variety of ethnic groups since first human habitation.

It is likely that Native American Indians used Harlem extensively before the arrival of the Dutch. In the winter, Manhattan offered insufficient shelter from the elements, but during the warm weather months the Lenape peoples, including Manahates and Wiechquaesecks, occupied hunting and fishing camps and also planted crops at various sites in northern Manhattan and elsewhere. Dutch explorers were startled to find grasslands in the area they later named Harlem—a result of native people's use of controlled fires to clear the land.

The sparse habitations of the Indians gradually gave way to Dutch farms. The director general of New Netherland, Petrus Stuyvesant, established Nieuw Haarlem in 1657. Located some ten miles north of the newly chartered city of New Amsterdam at Manhattan's southern tip, it was a tiny village clustered around today's East 121st and East 125th Streets on the shores of the Harlem River.

One hundred and fifty years later, the area was still largely agricultural. At the beginning of the nineteenth century, the village of Harlem in the eastern portion of the district comprised 91 families, one church, one school, and one library. Country estates dotted the landscape throughout the district, and Harlem Lane, which roughly corresponded to today's St. Nicholas Avenue, was a favorite racing venue for New York horse enthusiasts.

The eastern section of Harlem was developed earliest and had its own distinctive character. With the extension

BELOW Harlem Lane, roughly corresponding to today's St. Nicholas Avenue, running from Central Park to the village of Manhattanville, was a favorite horse-racing venue for nineteenth-century New York. The white steeple of St. Mary's Church in Manhattanville is visible on the left.

of the Third Avenue elevated railway to the area in 1879, blocks of tenements arose to accommodate unprecedented numbers of immigrants, mostly Italians (their settlement around Pleasant Avenue and East 116th Street was at one time the largest "Little Italy" in the United States) and Eastern European Jews. After Puerto Rico had become a US possession in 1898, and especially after the 1917 Jones Act had nationalized all Puerto Ricans as American citizens, Puerto Ricans began to leave the island and move stateside. The numbers grew after the Second World War, as natural disasters and changes in Puerto Rico's economy pushed Puerto Ricans from their island home. By the late 1940s, the eastern part of Harlem's cheap housing, ease of transportation, and tradition of labor organization established by the earlier Italian and Jewish arrivals—more than half of stateside Puerto Rican workers belonged to unions—attracted the majority of Puerto Rican migrants. The names "East Harlem" and "Spanish Harlem" began

to be applied to the district and, in its center, the largest stateside Puerto Rican settlement was called simply El Barrio ("the neighborhood").

Meanwhile, to the west, by the 1870s the Harlem and Hudson River railroads, along with the elevated train on Eighth Avenue (soon to be joined by a trolley car route along Amsterdam Avenue) attracted enough residents to give this section a more suburban character. Late in the 1880s, plans for the construction of a long-anticipated subway line (completed in 1904) unleashed a spate of land speculation and building. Overbuilding, combined with a national recession in the early twentieth century, yielded a glut of empty apartments, and developers reluctantly began to rent those apartments to African Americans desperate for new housing. The African Americans arrived from Manhattan's traditional black population centers— Greenwich Village and central West Side neighborhoods with colorful names such as the Tenderloin and San Juan

Hill—and, in ever greater numbers, from the segregated American South. By the 1920s, Harlem was becoming the fabled cultural capital of black America, its population booming, its critical mass of African Americans leading to a sense of pride (the term coined was the "New Negro"), the cross-pollination of ideas among established urbanites and newcomers from the American South and the Caribbean giving rise to new forms of literature and music—a flowering that became known as the Harlem Renaissance.

Writers flocked to Harlem—Langston Hughes to write poetry that employed the rhythms of African American music, especially blues and jazz; Zora Neale Hurston to publish stories based on Southern black folklore. Together, they formed the Harlem Suitcase Theater to present plays to ordinary people. Composer and band leader Duke Ellington, pianist Fats Waller, and many other musicians, as well as singers such as Billie Holiday and Ella Fitzgerald, elaborated on the rhythms of early jazz—America's first major contribution to world music—to produce exciting new sounds. Many performers got their first big break on the stage of the Apollo Theater on 125th Street in Harlem, the place in New York to catch the most exciting new American entertainment.

The Great Depression took some of the shine off Harlem, whose population suffered disproportionately because of racism and lack of opportunity. Forty years later, during New York City's fiscal crisis of the 1970s, both Harlem and Spanish Harlem were plagued by disinvestment and assaulted by the scourge of drugs; they did not emerge

from their own local depressions until the end of the twentieth century. Yet the generation of African Americans and Puerto Ricans that came of age during the 1960s and 1970s proudly embraced their heritage, created new Afro-Caribbean cultural forms, such as salsa, and established new cultural institutions, such as the Studio Museum in Harlem and El Museo del Barrio, which began on the Upper West Side but soon relocated to Spanish Harlem. And, in Harlem and other inner-city neighborhoods devastated by unemployment and urban decline, a young generation began to develop a defiant urban style called hip-hop, which combined graffiti, break dancing, deejaying, and emceeing (rapping), and quickly became a world style.

Beginning in the 1990s, Harlem and then East Harlem began to experience new investment and new population shifts. Both neighborhoods became more attractive to non-Latin whites looking for affordable housing close to Manhattan's midtown and downtown commercial districts. Harlem remains largely African American, but its lower socioeconomic classes struggle to afford to live there and all classes of black Harlemites worry that the neighborhood will one day cease to be the cultural capital of black America. East Harlem, now home to families from Mexico, the Dominican Republic, other Latin American countries, Africa, and elsewhere, is Upper Manhattan's most diverse community, its remaining Puerto Rican residents determined that the neighborhood must retain its storied past as the cradle of the stateside Puerto Rican community.

ABOVE, LEFT A scene from *Carolyn Capers*, a 1934 theatrical production by employees of the Carolyn Laundry at 111 East 128th Street in East Harlem.

ABOVE Joseph Rodriguez's 1987 photograph captures a game of "skelly" in East Harlem. Skelly, one of the classic New York City street games, is played with bottle caps that are flicked to skim across a board chalked or painted on the street's surface.

OPPOSITE Legendary jazz composer, pianist, and band leader "Duke" (Edward Kennedy) Ellington (1899–1974) with his orchestra, photographed in 1925. In a career spanning over 50 years, Ellington dabbled in a range of genres, and left behind a wealth of classic jazz numbers.

"TAKE THE 'A' TRAIN"

Of all the songs written about Harlem, probably none is more famous than the jazz standard "Take the 'A' Train." With music composed by Billy Strayhorn, who collaborated with bandleader Duke Ellington on countless musical compositions, the piece was first recorded in 1941 and quickly became the Ellington band's signature tune. A 17-year-old singer named Joya Sherrill heard the tune on the radio and wrote lyrics for it. Through a mutual friend, her father arranged for her to meet Ellington so she could sing him the lyrics she had written. Ellington adapted the lyrics and hired Sherrill as a vocalist with his band in 1942, six months after she had graduated from high school. The lyrics celebrate the IND subway line's express train.

Take Me Out to the Ball Game

As professional sports came of age in the twentieth century, New York's public culture was defined in part by its sport teams and the enthusiasm of its fans. Five Major League baseball teams and nine Negro League teams called New York home over the course of the century, as did no fewer than 17 professional football teams, both men's and women's professional basketball teams, and athletes from professional tennis, boxing, soccer, ice hockey, and many other sports.

Baseball mania dominated for much of the century, mainly because of complex and competing team loyalties. For more than 50 years, New York had the unique distinction of having three Major League teams in a single city, with the unprecedented situation of two of them playing in the same league. With the Brooklyn Dodgers and the New York Giants competing annually for the National League pennant, the rivalry was fierce—and the fans shared in it. There were 22 games a season in which the hometown teams played each other, either at the Polo Grounds in Manhattan or at Ebbets Field in Brooklyn, and the fans despised each other with a passion. There was an undercurrent to this: a social and cultural struggle between the multiethnic, multiracial, working-class underdog spirit of Brooklyn and the genteel, upper-crust image of the Giants' franchise.

One or the other of these teams often faced the New York Yankees in the World Series. The Yankees had become a powerhouse in the 1920s at the time when baseball first became a credible commercial enterprise, with a stellar lineup anchored at the start of the era by Babe Ruth (the team's new stadium in the Bronx was known as "the House that Ruth Built") and then enhanced by the likes of Lou Gherig and Joe DiMaggio. The Dodgers, long beloved in Brooklyn, became superstars in 1947 when they became the first modern Major League team to sign an African-American player, Jackie Robinson. Robinson, a star athlete at UCLA who had participated in football, baseball, and track in college, helped lead the team to its only World Series victory in 1955. Yet, just two years later, Brooklynites' hearts were broken when the team departed for California, along with the Giants. Many New Yorkers never forgave the owners, Horace Stoneham of the Giants and particularly Walter O'Malley of the Dodgers, for uprooting the teams, and especially for depriving Brooklyn of its beloved Dodgers.

There was some consolation in 1962, when the expansion of the National League opened an opportunity

OPPOSITE The Polo Grounds, designed by architect Henry B. Herts, were built in 1911 at West 157th Street and Harlem River Speedway. A burgeoning population, increased by the arrival of subway lines, joined fans from across the city to watch the New York Yankees (to 1923), the baseball Giants (to 1957), the football Giants (1925–55), and the New York Mets (1962–63). The stadium was demolished in 1964.

ABOVE Reformer and amateur photographer Jacob Riis captured this image of a boys' ball team at a playground on the Lower West Side of Manhattan in 1895, no doubt to call attention to the dreadful conditions in which city children of the poorer classes had to play. Not a blade of grass is evident in what looks more like a prison yard than a playground. Yet the image is timeless.

to create a new team, the New York Mets (short for Metropolitans). The Mets provided a home for many bereaved fans of the Dodgers and the Giants, as well as continuity with New York's National League heritage. Many players formerly with the Brooklyn Dodgers or New York Giants came to play for the young franchise. The Mets soon took up residence in the newly built Shea Stadium in Queens (since replaced by Citi Field) and created a miracle of their own in 1969 when they beat the Yankees to take the World Series.

Coincidentally, 1969 was also a championship year for the young New York Jets football team, led by the colorful quarterback-cum-celebrity, Joe Namath. The voyage of New York football toward becoming a professional sport had taken a rather different route to that of baseball. New York traced its football history most centrally through dominant college teams, who

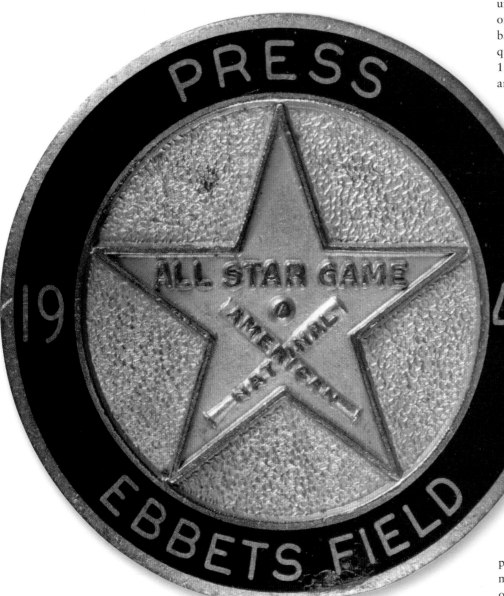

PRESS
19 ALL STAR GAME 49
AMERICAN
NATIONAL
EBBETS FIELD

began to gain huge followings in the late nineteenth century, when there were also games held between teams from outside the city who chose to play in New York. The city's first professional football team did not come into being until 1921, with the formation of the short-lived Brickley's Giants; in 1925, the New York Giants were formed, sharing a stadium—the Polo Grounds in Upper Manhattan—with the baseball Giants. The sport remained dominated by college play until after the Second World War, when the reputation of the football Giants grew, particularly after the baseball Giants and Dodgers left the city, partially quelling the city's baseball fever for a time. By the 1950s, with Frank Gifford as a star both on the field and in advertising, the football Giants were a major presence. The Jets came on the scene in the 1960s, and although both the Jets and the Giants now play in New Jersey, they are still considered hometown heroes by their New York fans.

The trajectory for professional basketball took yet another path. Traditionally an inner-city sport played by the urban poor in playgrounds, it was dominated by Jewish players throughout the 1930s and then increasingly by African Americans in the postwar era. College hoops were particularly popular, and the legendary City College squad of 1950 became the only men's team in history to win both the NCAA and National Invitation college championships in one year. The following year, the city was shocked when seven of the players were booked on bribery and conspiracy charges in a point-shaving scandal. By the beginning of the twenty-first century, the New York Knicks and the New York Liberty (a women's team) were both playing at Madison Square Garden, while a major and controversial campaign was underway to move the New Jersey Nets to New York in a new stadium planned near downtown Brooklyn.

Among the many other sports that have been played professionally in New York, one deserves special mention. The first tennis games in America were played on Staten Island in 1874, imported by Mary Ewing Outerbridge to the Staten Island cricket club. In 1915, the US National Championship was played in Forest Hills in Queens; it became the US Open in 1968, when the winner was a young African-American player named Arthur Ashe, for whom the stadium in which the Open is now held is named. His example, and that of many other players, spurred New York kids to take up tennis in the city's parks and courts, alongside games such as stickball, stoopball, racketball, and skating, which have haped the city's play over time.

OPPOSITE This badge was issued to members of the press who covered the 1949 All Star Game at Brooklyn's Ebbets Field, the ballpark that served as home of the Brooklyn Dodgers from April 1913 to September 1957. The ballpark was named for Dodgers' owner Charles Ebbets, who purchased the land over time and erected a facility seating 18,000 people. After the 1957 season, the Dodgers relocated to Los Angeles; the ballpark was torn down in 1960 to make way for housing.

BELOW On November 4, 2009, the New York Yankees celebrated their 7–3 win against the Philadelphia Phillies in Game Six of the 2009 MLB baseball World Series at the Yankee Stadium in the Bronx.

NEW YORK CENTRAL
& HUDSON RIVER RAILROAD.

5 GREAT LIMITED TRAINS 5

The NEW YORK CENTRAL is distinguished as the only line in America running Five Great Limited Trains to the West every day in the year, presenting a superb service uniformly correct in every detail. Following is the order of their departure from Grand Central Station **FOR THE GREAT CITIES OF THE WEST:**

THE **EMPIRE STATE** EXPRESS. NO EXTRA FARE.	At 9.00 a. m. every day, except Sunday; arrive at Buffalo 5.40 p. m., Niagara Falls 6.35 p. m. "THE FASTEST REGULAR PASSENGER TRAIN IN THE WORLD."—(62½ Miles an Hour.)
THE **CHICAGO** LIMITED.	At 10.00 a. m. every day, 138th Street 10.09 a. m., arriving at Chicago 9.45 a. m. next day, via the Lake Shore. "THE FAST MAIL ROUTE."
THE **SOUTHWESTERN** LIMITED. NO EXTRA FARE.	At 1.30 p. m. every day, 138th Street 1.40 p. m., arriving at Cincinnati 11.20 a. m., Indianapolis 11.55 a. m., St. Louis 7.15 p m. next day, via "THE BIG FOUR ROUTE."
THE **WORLD'S FAIR** SPECIAL NO EXTRA FARE	At 1.30 p. m. every day, 138th Street 1.40 p. m., arriving at Chicago 3.00 p. m. next day, via New York Central and Lake Shore. "THE FAST MAIL ROUTE."
THE **NORTH SHORE** LIMITED.	At 4.30 p. m. every day, arriving at Chicago 4.30 p. m. next day, via the Michigan Central. "THE NIAGARA FALLS ROUTE."

In addition to the above magnificent service. the New York Central has eleven other daily trains across the Empire State, to the

NORTH AND WEST.

GEO. H. DANIELS, Gen'l Passenger Agent, Grand Central Depot.   MILTON C. ROACH, Gen'l Eastern Pass. Agent, Broadway, New York.

SEIDENBERG & CO.'S LA ROSA ESPANOLA. Famous Key West Havana Cigars, all Vuelta Abajo.

THE NATIONAL LEAGUE AND American Association OF PROFESSIONAL BASE BALL CLUBS.

First Division, April 12th to July 13th.

THE NATIONAL BOARD.

CHAS. H. BYRNE, President, Brooklyn, N. Y.
N. E. YOUNG, Secretary and Treasurer, Washington, D. C.
ZACH PHELPS, Louisville, Ky.

LEAGUE PRESIDENTS.

FRANK DE HAAS ROBISON, Cleveland.
JAMES HART, Chicago.
CHRIS. VON DER AHE, St. Louis.
DR. STUCKY, Louisville.
JOHN T. BRUSH, Cincinnati.
W. C. TEMPLE, Pittsburgh.
JOHN B. DAY, New York.
A. H. SODEN, Boston.
HARRY VON DER HORST, Baltimore.
GEORGE WAGNER, Washington.
A. J. REACH, Philadelphia.
CHARLES H. BYRNE, Brooklyn.

League Club Managers.

Patrick Powers	New York
John M. Ward	Brooklyn
Frank Selee	Boston
Harry Wright	Philadelphia
Adrian C. Anson	Chicago
Charles Comiskey	Cincinnati
George Van Haltren	Baltimore
	Washington
Albert Buckenberger	Pittsburg
Oliver Tebeau	Cleveland
John Chapman	Louisville
John Glasscock	St. Louis

League Club Captains.

William Ewing	New York
John M. Ward	Brooklyn
John Clements	Philadelphia
William Nash	Boston
A. C. Anson	Chicago
Edward Hanlon	Pittsburg
John Glasscock	St. Louis
Fred Pfeiffer	Louisville
Oliver Tebeau	Cleveland
Charles Comiskey	Cincinnati
Dan Richardson	Washington
George Van Haltren	Baltimore

NEW YORK AT HOME.

FIRST DIVISION.

April 21	Washington
22	Washington
23	Washington
25	Boston
26	Philadelphia
May 14	Philadelphia
16	Baltimore
17	Baltimore
18	Baltimore
25	Chicago
26	Chicago
27	Chicago
28	St. Louis
30	St. Louis
31	St. Louis
June 2	Pittsburg
3	Pittsburg
4	Louisville
6	Louisville
7	Louisville
8	Cincinnati
9	Cincinnati
10	Cincinnati
13	Cleveland
14	Cleveland
15	Cleveland
16	Brooklyn
17	Brooklyn
18	Brooklyn
23	Philadelphia
24	Philadelphia
25	Boston
27	Boston

SECOND DIVISION.

July 11	Pittsburg
12	Pittsburg
13	Cincinnati
19	Cincinnati
20	Chicago
22	Chicago
23	St. Louis
25	St. Louis
26	Cleveland
27	Cleveland
28	Louisville
29	Louisville
30	Brooklyn
Aug. 3	Brooklyn
5	Washington
6	Washington
8	Baltimore
10	Baltimore
18	Chicago
20	Chicago
22	Pittsburg
23	Pittsburg
24	Cincinnati
25	Cincinnati
26	St. Louis
27	St. Louis
29	Louisville
30	Louisville
31	Cleveland
Sept. 1	Cleveland
2	Boston
3	Boston
5	Boston
7	Philadelphia
8	Philadelphia
9	Washington
10	Washington
12	Brooklyn
13	Brooklyn
14	Baltimore
15	Baltimore
Oct. 1	Philadelphia
3	Washington
4	Washington
5	Brooklyn
6	Brooklyn
11	Baltimore
12	Baltimore

THE SPORTING PRESS

The city's newspapers helped to make New York sports more commercialized and professional. As far back as the 1820s, papers such as the *New York Clipper* and the *Spirit of the Times* began covering racing and trotting as well as the new sport of baseball. By the 1890s, newspaper owners recognized the growing popularity of professional sports and many began devoting a whole page to the city's sports teams. Newspaper coverage of baseball, football, and basketball helped bring these sports to prominence and shift New Yorkers' attention away from the more informal sporting activities of the nineteenth century.

Sports coverage also increased the circulation and profits of the newspapers. By the middle of the twentieth century, the New York region had more than a dozen newspapers—four morning papers (the *Daily Mirror*, the *Daily News*, the *Herald Tribune*, and the *Times*); three afternoon papers (the *World–Telegram and Sun*, the *Journal–American*, and the *Post*); and out on "the Island," the *Long Island Press*, *Newsday*, and the *Brooklyn Eagle*. Sports reporters such as Frank Graham and Red Smith became minor celebrities and developed devoted readerships. Readers expected unique coverage of the local sports teams, so ten of the papers sent reporters on the road with the city's baseball clubs. Many households made a daily habit of purchasing two or three papers, just to read the differing coverage of a game.

LEFT The New York Ball Club was part of the National League and American Association of Professional Base Ball Clubs. The list of New York players includes an O'Rourke, who quite possibly was James Henry O'Rourke, known as "Orator Jim," whose celebrated professional career spanned the years 1876 to 1892.

New York at War

The military history of America's great city began as early as the 1640s, when Dutch soldiers and militia fought the local Lenape Indians. Following the English conquest of New Amsterdam in 1664, New Yorkers sailed as armed privateers against the French and Spanish in several colonial wars. During the American Revolution, General Howe captured the city in 1776 for King George III. The British did

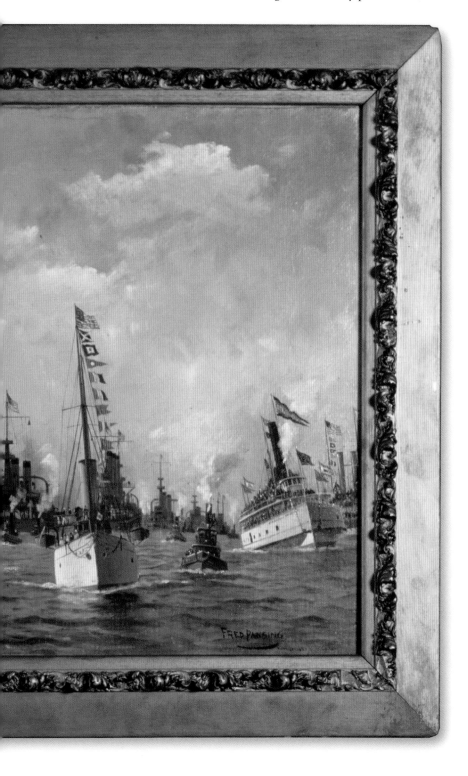

not have to relinquish control of the city until the war concluded seven years later and they evacuated New York on November 25, 1783.

New York was at the eye of the nation's military storms throughout the nineteenth and twentieth centuries. The city, now the nation's biggest port and its center of finance and business, as well as the point of embarkation for many of the nation's troops being sent overseas, frequently found itself at the center of mobilization—and of the controversies—surrounding America's foreign and military policies.

The strategic importance of New York harbor made the city keenly nervous about its own vulnerability to attack. It was in the period preceding America's next conflict with the British, the War of 1812, that New York added four forts to its strategic inventory, including Castle William on Governors Island and Castle Clinton, originally off the southern shore of Manhattan but later joined to the island through landfill. (Castle Clinton, later renamed Castle Garden, would go on to have a storied and colorful life as, in sequence, a concert hall, the point of arrival for immigrants in the pre-Ellis Island days, an aquarium, and as a ticketing point for visiting the Statue of Liberty and Ellis Island.)

The Civil War showed clearly that the threat from within could be as serious as the threat from overseas. The city was deeply divided over the Confederate cause. While many New Yorkers fought for the abolition of slavery and eagerly volunteered for military service, many of the leading merchants were closely allied with Southern planters, who supplied lucrative cotton—the "white gold" that they then sent around the world. These so-called "Copperheads" bitterly opposed the war to preserve the Union, even going so far as to agitate for New York City itself seceding and becoming its own independent state, free to trade with whom it would.

The sharpest dissent from the war effort came from immigrant workers, who worried that the end of slavery would flood the market with cheap African-American labor and drive down their wages. They also particularly resented the policy on the draft, which allowed men with sufficient resources to buy their way out of military service, turning the conflict into "a rich man's war and a poor man's fight." On July 13, 1863, some of the worst rioting in the nation's history broke out at the Ninth District draft office at Third Avenue and 47th Street. Unleashing their fury on black New Yorkers, the rioters turned the city into a war zone of its own, burning down not only the draft office, but also the city's Colored Orphan Asylum. At the end of New York's Civil War draft riots, at least 105 lay dead, and an estimated $3–5 million-worth of property lay in ruins.

The great conflicts of the twentieth century were fought far away from New York. During the First World War, as an article in *Vanity Fair* described, "The war has not hit [New York] as it has hit London, or Paris, or Rome. Here life is still more or less normal, there are still cakes and ale—in spite of Mr. Hoover—and ginger is still hot i' the mouth." But that war divided New Yorkers, pitting self-styled "100% Americans" against German immigrants, pacifists, leftists, and anyone else who dared question the war effort.

The Second World War brought rationing, nighttime dimouts, hundreds of thousands of troops swarming the streets and thronging to the Stage Door Canteen to enjoy free food and free shows by the biggest stars of the day, and an iconic VJ Day celebration in Times Square. All of these made New York City one of the emblems of the war effort. But even more notably, the Second World War, while wreaking its devastating effects on cities in Europe, ushered in a period when New York emerged for the first time as an undisputed world capital. As the great French architect Le Corbusier wrote of the city in 1947, "Today it belongs to the world. Without anyone expecting it, it has become the jewel in the crown of universal cities."

The optimism of this post-Second World War era faded, however, as hard times hit the city in the 1960s and 1970s, and another—much more controversial—war again tore New Yorkers apart. The conflict in Vietnam set New York's streets, parks, and campuses reeling. Hundreds of thousands flocked to the antiwar rallies including the Moratorium in October 1969, but supporters of the war rallied too, and the groups clashed in the so-called "hard hat riot" on May 8, 1970, when construction workers attacked antiwar demonstrators in the streets of Lower Manhattan. Major John V. Lindsay saw the war as an urban issue, arguing that it siphoned off billions of dollars from

BELOW New York's Seventh Regiment National Guard, formed in 1847, was known as the "silk stocking regiment" because a large number of its members belonged to the city's elite. By the 1860s it had more than 1,000 members. The regiment served the Union cause during the Civil War and was called to New York City to help quell the Draft Riots of July 13, 1863, the occasion of this photograph.

desperately needed social programs, and he emerged as a national political figure in the antiwar movement.

New York's most recent and most gruesome experience with an undeclared war came in 2001, when a coordinated terrorist attack destroyed the city's iconic Twin Towers. As smoke and ash billowed through the streets for days after the tragedy, New Yorkers—and Americans—united perhaps more closely than ever before. "Tomorrow New York is going to be here," declared Mayor Rudolph Giuliani. "And we're going to rebuild, and we're going to be stronger than we

were before … I want the people of New York to be an example to the rest of the country, and the rest of the world, that terrorism can't stop us."

ABOVE The First World War Victory Arch at Fifth Avenue and 24th Street was erected in 1919 to honor the city's war dead. Architect Thomas Hastings fashioned the arch of wood and plaster, on the assumption that it would later be rebuilt of more permanent materials. Conflicts over who would build and who would pay for the permanent arch doomed that project, and the temporary arch was eventually demolished.

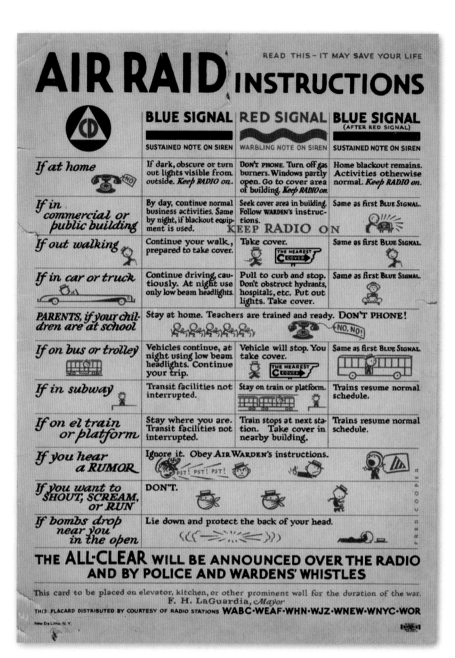

AIR RAID INSTRUCTIONS

READ THIS - IT MAY SAVE YOUR LIFE

	BLUE SIGNAL — SUSTAINED NOTE ON SIREN	RED SIGNAL ～ WARBLING NOTE ON SIREN	BLUE SIGNAL (AFTER RED SIGNAL) — SUSTAINED NOTE ON SIREN
If at home	If dark, obscure or turn out lights visible from outside. *Keep RADIO on.*	DON'T PHONE. Turn off gas burners. Windows partly open. Go to cover area of building. *Keep RADIO on.*	Home blackout remains. Activities otherwise normal. *Keep RADIO on.*
If in commercial or public building	By day, continue normal business activities. Same by night, if blackout equipment is used. KEEP RADIO ON	Seek cover area in building. Follow WARDEN's instructions.	Same as first BLUE SIGNAL.
If out walking	Continue your walk, prepared to take cover.	Take cover. THE NEAREST COVER	Same as first BLUE SIGNAL.
If in car or truck	Continue driving, cautiously. At night use only low beam headlights.	Pull to curb and stop. Don't obstruct hydrants, hospitals, etc. Put out lights. Take cover.	Same as first BLUE SIGNAL.
PARENTS, if your children are at school	Stay at home. Teachers are trained and ready. DON'T PHONE!		
If on bus or trolley	Vehicles continue, at night using low beam headlights. Continue your trip.	Vehicle will stop. You take cover. THE NEAREST COVER	Same as first BLUE SIGNAL.
If in subway	Transit facilities not interrupted.	Stay on train or platform.	Trains resume normal schedule.
If on el train or platform	Stay where you are. Transit facilities not interrupted.	Train stops at next station. Take cover in nearby building.	Trains resume normal schedule.
If you hear a RUMOR	Ignore it. Obey AIR WARDEN's instructions.		
If you want to SHOUT, SCREAM, or RUN	DON'T.		
If bombs drop near you in the open	Lie down and protect the back of your head.		

THE ALL-CLEAR WILL BE ANNOUNCED OVER THE RADIO AND BY POLICE AND WARDENS' WHISTLES

This card to be placed on elevator, kitchen, or other prominent wall for the duration of the war.
F. H. LaGuardia, *Mayor*
THIS PLACARD DISTRIBUTED BY COURTESY OF RADIO STATIONS WABC·WEAF·WHN·WJZ·WNEW·WNYC·WOR

New Era Litho. N.Y.

FRED COOPER

OPPOSITE An aerial view of Levittown, Long Island, New York. The new suburb of regularly spaced and shaped dwellings was built at extaordinary speed to alleviate the housing shortage in the aftermath of the Second World War.

ABOVE New York's security precautions during World War II included the dimming of Times Square's bright lights (they were intense enough to silhouette ships off Far Rockaway, heightening their visibility to German U-boat attack) and frequent air raid drills. This placard, to be placed in a prominent location in people's homes, instructed New Yorkers on what to do in the event of an air raid.

AFTER THE WAR WAS OVER

The end of the Second World War ushered in a period of optimism and prosperity in the United States—but also the seeds of a long era of urban decline. The GI Bill, which opened the way to college and home ownership for millions of veterans, also paved the way to the suburbs, as new developments, such as Levittown on Long Island, were built with dazzling speed to address the postwar housing shortage. The road to the suburbs was literally paved by the Federal government, whose Interstate Highway initiative provided the infrastructure for the growth of a regional economy and the growth of bedroom communities not only on Long Island, but in New Jersey, Connecticut, Westchester, and beyond. Some predicted that the era of the city was over; however, new arrivals and committed city residents ultimately proved that reports of New York's demise were premature, and in the twenty-first century, the city is bigger and more populous than ever.

City of Arts

Today New York City is the center of the American (and arguably the global) art world, a leader in both visual and performing arts. But it was not always so. In fact, New York—in its early years more associated with the quest to earn a buck than with the transcendence of art—struggled to establish itself as something greater than a center of raw materialism. It emerged only gradually as a force to be reckoned with on the world art scene. Four key moments across two centuries help to illustrate how this came to pass—as well as the creative dynamic of cross-fertilization among the fine arts and performing arts that helps to propel New York's cultural dominance.

One turning point was 1870, the year of the establishment of the Metropolitan Museum of Art. In the early days of the Republic, New York had worked to define itself as a credible focal point for the arts, surpassing Philadelphia as the center of American design. The National Academy of Design, founded in New York in 1825, had created a locus for visual arts in the city through the establishment of the first American art school; the city even got its own orchestra, the New York Philharmonic Society, in 1842. But New York emerged from the Civil War with a strong feeling that it needed to create an art scene worthy of a world capital, in order to compete with the great European cities. The resulting impulse created not only the Metropolitan Museum of Art (where New York's Hudson River School painters exhibited breathtaking American landscapes alongside the work of European artists), but also a dazzling array of other cultural institutions and organizations. These included the artists' group named the Salmagundi Club (1871), Oratorio Society of New York (1871), the Art Students' League (1875), the Society of American Artists (1877), the New York Symphony Society (1878), the Metropolitan Opera (1883), and Carnegie Hall (1891). These and many others joined antebellum institutions such as the Brooklyn Academy of Music (1861) to present the civilizing influence of European-style fine art, music, and dance.

Less than 50 years later, everything seemed to be in flux. In 1913, Americans were still looking to Europe, but this time for avant-garde art, rather than for the reassuring stability of the academic traditions. That was the year of the landmark "Armory Show" in New York—the "First International Exhibition of Modern Art in America" which introduced New Yorkers to European modernism. Among the committee who organized the show were members of the so-called "Ashcan School," including Robert Henri and John

Sloan, who explored the realities of modern urban life in paintings and prints. Another key force was the pioneering photographer Alfred Stieglitz, who, just five years earlier, had opened 291, a gallery on Fifth Avenue that exhibited modern art in all media. Meanwhile, dancers such as Isadora Duncan and Ruth St. Denis, celebrated among this group of artists, were experimenting with new forms of modern dance. On the popular dance floor, ragtime was in vogue, and Vernon and Irene Castle were introducing New Yorkers to new

ABOVE The new building to which this 1894 invitation refers was the Metropolitan Museum of Art's grand entrance wing on Fifth Avenue, designed in the Beaux-Arts style by Richard Morris Hunt. Henry G. Marquand was the second president of the museum and a major donor to its collections.

ballroom dance crazes that broke all of the established rules of Victorian propriety. Charles Ives experimented with radically new forms of dissonant music, starting with "Central Park in the Dark,"inspired by the sounds of Manhattan. The New York arts world seemed to be living proof of Virginia Woolf's declaration that "on or about December 1910, human character changed."

By 1948, the year that Jackson Pollock first exhibited his "drip paintings" at the Betty Parsons Gallery on East 57th Street, revolution was in the air again. The multidisciplinary artistic movements of the Harlem Renaissance of the 1920s and 1930s had helped to create a new American voice in music, dance, prose, and poetry. The years leading to the Second World War had brought an influx of European artists and intellectuals who were fleeing fascism and the devastation of the war, and they brought with them new versions of the avant-garde. In

New York, they rubbed elbows with the young American artists raised on the ideas presented at the Armory Show, and together they created the New York School—a cross-disciplinary movement that encompassed Abstract Expressionist painting, experimental music, postmodern dance, and avant-garde poetry. The movement resonated with and drew inspiration from new artistic forces in postwar New York, including Beat poetry and bebop jazz. This all added up to a heady artistic and intellectual atmosphere in which painters such as Willem DeKooning, Jackson Pollock, Lee Krasner, and Mark Rothko mingled with other creative people such as the sculptors Louise Bourgeois and Isamu Noguchi, poets John Ashbery and Frank O'Hara, choreographers Merce Cunningham and Martha Graham, composer John Cage, musicians Miles Davis, Thelonius Monk, and Charlie Parker, and photographers Robert Frank, Fred McDarrah, and

Aaron Siskind, exchanging ideas at places such as the Cedar Tavern on University Place in the Village. For the first time, the momentum of the modern art world had definitively shifted from Paris to New York; at the end of 1948, painter Barnett Newman defined the sublime in art by arguing: "I believe that here in America, some of us, free from the weight of European culture, are finding the answer, by completely denying that art has any concern with the problem of beauty and where to find it."

In the late 1970s, a different dynamic was defining an utterly new New York "school." What is now known as "old school" (or "old skool") hip-hop emerged from the streets of Harlem, the South Bronx, and Brooklyn at a time when these neighborhoods were hit badly by neglect, economic downturns, and urban blight. Like the New York School of the 1950s, New York hip-hop combined music, art, dance, and the spoken word—but this time in a defiant, outspoken, and decidedly urban style. In basketball courts and neighborhood parks, black and Latino youth forged the elements of what would become hip-hop: graffiti, b-boying (break dancing), deejaying (or scratching), emceeing (rapping), sampling, beatboxing, and along with them new styles of dress and self-expression. Led by pioneers such as DJ Kool Herc, Afrika Bambaataa, Grandmaster Flash and the Furious Five (member Keith Cowboy is often credited for coining the term "hip-hop"), and the Sugarhill Gang, who released the first hip-hop recording, "Rapper's Delight," in 1979, East Coast hip-hop channeled the energy of everyday life in New York City's concrete jungle and produced a style that is wholly distinct to the region. By the late twentieth century, it was the most influential cultural export of the United States and the most important— and most lucrative—global style in the world.

OPPOSITE This advertisement promoted the business of Currier & Ives, which made "engravings for the people." The firm employed a staff of artists, lithographers, and hand colorists, who produced the art work in assembly-line fashion.

BELOW The first Metropolitan Opera house, at Broadway and 39th Street, opened in 1883, presenting standard operas, all sung in Italian. In this 1944 photograph, all of its 3,700 seats appear to be filled. Its appeal did not diminish when it moved uptown to the new Lincoln Center for the Performing Arts in 1966.

In nineteenth-century New York, Currier & Ives, a firm based in New York and nicknamed "the Grand Central Depot for Cheap and Popular Prints," turned fine art paintings into hand-colored lithographs, thus creating art that was affordable for nearly anyone. From 1857 to 1907, the company founded by Nathaniel Currier and James Merritt Ives was spectacularly prolific, producing an average of three or four new prints on a wide variety of subjects every week for 50 years. All told, the firm, located in Lower Manhattan, produced millions of prints in unlimited editions from an inventory of over 7,000 titles. Currier & Ives's images of news events and political cartoons appealed to readers of the daily "penny presses," its decorative pictures cost less than engravings and "chromos," and its celebrity portraits and historical scenes offered color and movement beyond the means of early photography. A Currier & Ives "top-of-the-line" large-folio print cost from $1.50 to $3 and small-folio prints cost pennies, making the studio's prints exceptionally affordable. Currier & Ives's images could be seen in homes across America.

LEFT Construction began on May 14, 1959, for Philharmonic Hall, the first building at Lincoln Center for the Performing Arts, the 16.3-acre arts complex envisioned by John D. Rockefeller III and enabled by Robert Moses's urban renewal program. The complex now houses 12 arts organizations. Philharmonic Hall was renamed Avery Fisher Hall in 1973.

BELOW "Red Cube", a 1968 sculpture
by Isamu Noguchi that sits on Broadway,
between Liberty and Cedar Streets, in
New York's financial district.

The Literary Trade

New York has long proved a magnet for writers, drawn by the city's vibrant cultural and street life, dynamic concentrated publishing industry, and community of other writers. But the phases and varieties of its literary history are so vast as to defy easy categorization or chronology. Most historians agree that its origins go back to the early nineteenth century, when Washington Irving helped to create the popular image of New York's colonial past and its emerging identity through his first major work, the satirical *A History of New York from the Beginning of the World to the End of the Dutch Dynasty*. Along with James Fenimore Cooper, who lived for several years in New York City, where he penned *The Last of the Mohicans*, Irving helped to create a newly American voice in literature.

Irving's generation was followed closely by a new, more experimental one. It included Edgar Allan Poe, who lived for a time in the Village, in what is now the Upper West Side, and in the Bronx; the critic Margaret Fuller; native New Yorker Herman Melville, who wrote several works, including his semiautobiographical *Bartleby the Scrivener*, in the city; and Walt Whitman,

who worked as a newspaperman (also serving as editor of the *Brooklyn Eagle*) and self-published the first of multiple editions of his collected poems under the title *Leaves of Grass* in New York. Poems of his such as "Crossing Brooklyn Ferry," drew inspiration from the daily experiences of city life.

Beginning in the late nineteenth century, writers of fiction turned their pens perceptively to the subject of life in the burgeoning metropolis. Henry James's *Washington Square*, Edith Wharton's *The Age of Innocence*, William Dean Howells' *A Hazard of New Fortunes*, Stephen Crane's *Maggie, A Girl of the Streets*, and Theodore Dreiser's *Sister Carrie* all shone a light on life in New York's Gilded Age, with its complex social mores, extremes of wealth and poverty, and its rapidly changing metropolitan dynamics.

By the 1920s, a fresh New York was emerging, sharply different from the Victorian city that James and his contemporaries had depicted. Transformed by immigration, the growth of corporate wealth, and a new, modern sensibility, this New York gave birth to diverse versions of twentieth-century literature. One strand was closely connected by a newly invigorated group of

OPPOSITE The interior of the Lotos Club, one of the oldest literary clubs in the United States, ca.1910. Formed in 1870, the Lotos Club of New York took both its name and motto from the first stanza of Alfred Lord Tennyson's 1832 poem "The Lotos-Eaters." The initially all-male club originally attracted a membership from the city's professional, literary, and academic spheres who welcomed a wide range of distinguished visitors to their banquets. One of the early members was Mark Twain, who called it "the Ace of Clubs."

RIGHT The Algonquin Hotel, West 44th Street, Manhattan, opened in 1902. For about a decade beginning in 1919, its Rose Room was a regular meeting place for glitterati writers, actors, and musicians. This photograph was taken in 2009.

121

literary magazines, beginning with the "little magazines" such as the *Dial* and the *Little Review*, published in the Village just before and after the First World War, and then embodied in the new journalism of *The New Yorker*. *The New Yorker's* brand of smart, ironic, urbane humor was exemplified in daily lunchtime gatherings at the Algonquin Hotel on 44th Street in Manhattan. Known as the "Algonquin Round Table," this group of writers, critics, playwrights, journalists, and actors, including Dorothy Parker, Edna Ferber, Harold Ross, Robert Benchley, and Alexander Woolcott, helped to create and personify the irreverent tone of the 1920s. Yet no single writer embodied the spirit of the era so indelibly as F. Scott Fitzgerald, whose books, such as *The Great Gatsby*, echoed the glamorous life that he and his wife Zelda led, and who coined the phrase "the Jazz Age."

At the same time, several miles north in Harlem, new literary ground was being broken as black writers such as James Weldon Johnson, Claude McKay, Zora Neale Hurston, and Langston Hughes found the voice of the "New Negro." Drawing inspiration from diverse sources, including jazz, Southern black traditions, and their own urban experience, they created a vibrant literary and cultural scene that explored themes such as alienation and exoticism. In philosopher Alain Locke's words, "Negro life is seizing upon its first chances for group expression and self-determination."

If the signature New York literary journal of 1920s was *The New Yorker*, the formative one of the Depression era and beyond was *Partisan Review*, which provided a symbolic home to a group of new intellectual writers, many of them inspired by the radical politics of the 1930s and brought up within the heady culture of debate of the City University in those years. They explored issues of sexuality, of the subconscious, and of political action, and frequently turned a critical eye on American society. During its almost 70-year existence, *Partisan Review* published works by Lillian Hellman, Mary McCarthy, Delmore Schwartz, James Agee, Saul Bellow, Norman Mailer, Susan Sontag, and many others. Along with

ABOVE In this picture from 1887, the New York poet Walt Whitman was 68 years old. His collection *Leaves of Grass* (1855) was inspired, he said, by "my life in Brooklyn and New York, absorbing a million people for fifteen years with an intimacy, eagerness, and abandon, probably never equaled."

later arrivals such as *The New York Review of Books*, these New York magazines founded in the 1920s and 1930s created the center of gravity in a disparate and multifaceted literary world.

By the late twentieth and early twenty-first centuries, no literary movement went unrepresented in the vibrant scene in New York City. The diversity of voices ranged from Tom Wolfe to Oscar Hijuelos, Frank McCourt, Toni Morrison, and Caleb Carr, all enlivening the city's, its presses, its literary journals, and the bookshelves of the world.

THE GREAT GATSBY

"The city seen from the Queensboro Bridge is always the city seen for the first time, in its first wild promise of all the mystery and the beauty in the world."—F. Scott Fitzgerald, *The Great Gatsby*

F. Scott Fitzgerald's most famous book, published in 1925, is set in post-First World War New York City and Long Island's North Shore. Its protagonist, Nick Carraway, is a Midwesterner of comfortable means who, after serving in the war, settles in New York City to "learn the bond business." The economy is soaring, Prohibition is in effect, and both the city and its wealthy North Shore suburbs are centers of money and excess. While living in a summer rental in a wealthy town called "West Egg," Carraway meets Jay Gatsby, his mysterious next door neighbor, and chronicles Gatsby's efforts to bridge the chasm between old money and new money.

Regarded as a seminal work on the fallibility of the American Dream, *The Great Gatsby* was in part autobiographical. A Midwesterner like Nick Carraway, Fitzgerald also both romanticized and criticized the excesses of New York in the Roaring Twenties. Like his protagonist, who became disgusted with life in New York and returned to the Midwest, Fitzgerald became disillusioned and moved to France two years after the novel's publication.

On the Runway

New York's role as the fashion capital of America is rooted in its history as the nation's premier producer of clothing. The city's garment manufacturers sowed the seeds of the clothing industry when they began making ready-to-wear men's apparel before the Civil War. By the middle of the nineteenth century, clothing production was already the largest manufacturing sector in the metropolis. But the watershed moment for the industry came in the early twentieth century: responding to the growing number of women in the labor force, manufacturers provided the new market with a supply of off-the-rack two-piece tailored suits, shirtwaist bodices, and skirts, ushering in the modern garment business. The garment industry would transform the economy, politics, culture, and built environment of the city, while New York, in turn, was poised to remake the way the world dressed. By the First World War, New York City was home to nearly two-thirds of the nation's garment manufacturers, many of them clustered on the Lower East Side. The wholesale firms that mass-produced ready-made clothing relied on the tailoring expertise, design inspiration, and plentiful labor of European immigrants. Some immigrants (especially German and Eastern European Jews) strove to set up their own businesses, while others (such as Italians) worked primarily as hired labor for already existing businesses. Many workers toiled in sweatshops, at home, or in poorly regulated and sometimes dangerous factory buildings, as dramatized by the tragic Triangle shirtwaist factory fire in 1911.

In the aftermath of that disastrous fire, reformers and unionists agitated for modern, safe facilities. Simultaneously, property and business owners along Fifth Avenue sought to segregate manufacturing from retail and residential areas, and to separate immigrant workers from upper-class residents and the shoppers who bought their goods. By the 1920s, these disparate agendas had coalesced in the creation of the Garment Center—hundreds of state-of-the-art factory loft buildings and showroom spaces in a 15-block area of midtown Manhattan. It was the world's first industrial park for apparel production, which was able to accommodate all of the industry's many parts—garment design and assembly; auxiliary industries such as fabric, embroidery, buttons, trimmings, notions, and sewing machine repairs; and merchandising—here were thousands of mostly small firms that operated and interacted as a complicated whole.

During the Second World War and the years immediately following, two forces converged to transform the New York garment industry into the New York fashion industry. The city's nexus of production and marketing, put in place before the war, reached a high point of efficiency and organization. Simultaneously, New York design came of age, having stepped into the vacuum left when French couture houses suspended operations during the war. The result was the reinvention of world fashion.

If any one event can be identified as the birth of New York City as a capital of international fashion it was the first Fashion Week in 1943. The event, organized by fashion legend Eleanor Lambert in an effort to legitimize American fashion and diminish American reliance on French fashion, provided American designers with an opportunity to display their most recent collections in a series of runway shows that would ultimately determine industry-wide trends. American fashion magazines—including *Vogue*, which had previously promoted American design but reserved judgment as to its ability to supersede Parisian chic—covered the event extensively. Since Fashion Week's trial run, New York has semi-annually played host to the country's most glamorous, highly publicized fashion extravaganzas,

RIGHT Until the 1930s, New Yorkers depended on Paris for both their personal wardrobes and fashion leadership. Charles Frederick Worth (born in Lincolnshire, England) and the Parisian couture house that he founded provided opulent attire for most of New York's "Gilded Age" families. This wedding dress, worn by Annie Schermerhorn in 1878, exemplifies the quality of design as well as materials for which Worth was famous.

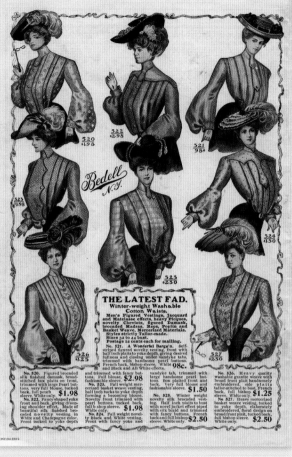

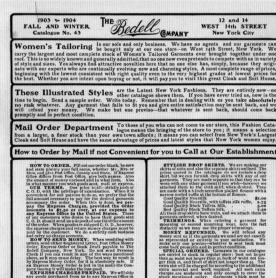

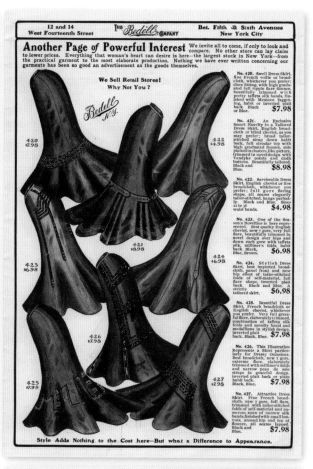

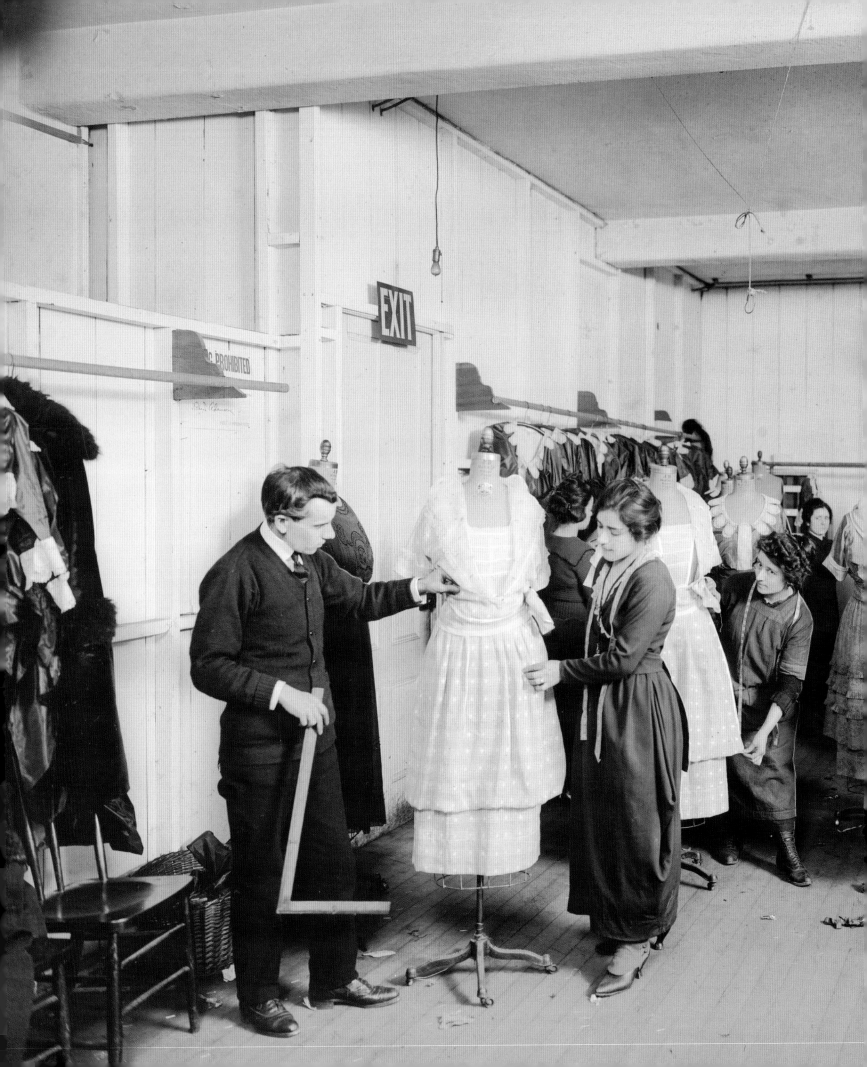

and witnessed its successful spread to each of the world's leading fashion capitals—London, Paris, and Milan.

The fresh new American styles introduced at that first Fashion Week invigorated the industry, giving rise to a new crop of talent lured by the prospect of actually designing under their own labels rather than producing anonymously. With the added incentive of Coty's Fashion Critics Award, also launched by Lambert, this new generation of New York-based innovators irrevocably weaned itself from the supremacy of Parisian leadership. Further galvanizing their identity as American fashion designers, 20 newly preeminent figures—including Bill Blass, Donald Brooks, Norman Norell, Arnold Scaasi, and Pauline Trigere—joined forces in 1962 to establish the Council of Fashion Designers of America (CFDA).

The first CFDA Awards ceremony was held in 1981, its glamour superseding the more modest Coty Awards and nurturing the powerful 1990s trend toward the rise of high-profile apparel companies. The branding and marketing techniques routinely engaged in by these new mega-businesses provided a new hierarchy of design leadership in the city, while effectively heralding the end of the era of the small wholesale manufacturer.

Dovetailing with this new garment industry dynamic, the early 1980s witnessed the birth of a fashion trend that emerged from the streets of New York: hip-hop style. With the popularization of its sport-inspired, unconstructed clothes, the new urban style unnerved the elders of the clothing industry and successfully challenged the supremacy of New York's fashion establishment. Suddenly, labels and clothing lines bore the iconic names of the stars of the new dynamic hip-hop culture, who had expanded their role from performer to designer and permanently altered the look of American clothing.

Today there are just 25,000 apparel workers in the Garment Center, working in 150 factories. Yet, while the assembling of clothing has moved abroad, the designers and company headquarters remain in New York. Designers, sample makers, salespeople, specialist contractors, and suppliers of all aesthetics continue to make New York their center of operations, maintaining New York's role as a world fashion city as well as a cultural capital.

LEFT The Joseph J. Keyser Company was located at 225 West 36th Street, in the area that had become New York City's garment district by the time this photograph was taken. Men and women are shown draping dress forms right on the floor of the factory.

VERSAILLES

American designers established their place in the global fashion world at a historic 1973 fashion show at the Palace of Versailles in France. There they challenged the supremacy of European design on its own turf. The five New York designers invited to show their collections—Bill Blass, Stephen Burrows, Oscar de la Renta, Halston, and Anne Klein—shook up the status quo and brought the French to their feet, cheering. And it was not only the American designs they cheered, but the American models, including a cohort of African-American models who strutted the designs of black designer Stephen Burrows with a pizzazz never before seen on a fashion runway.

OPPOSITE During the 1930s and 1940s, Bond Clothes was the largest retail chain of men's clothing in the United States, best known for selling two-pant suits. The Bond Clothing Store at 1530 Broadway in Times Square, opened in 1940, was called "the cathedral of clothing." The store closed in 1977.

LEFT Anne Klein pants suits, modeled at a fire station in New York, October 3, 1972.

Media Capital

Times Square = *The New York Times.* Herald Square = The *New York Herald.* Madison Avenue = advertising. The landscape of New York, America's media capital, is peppered with the history of journalism and media. But before there was Times Square, Herald Square, or an advertising industry on Madison Avenue, there was another media center: Newspaper Row, a five-block stretch along the east side of City Hall Park, where dozens of publishers and printers set up shop in the 1840s as New York's newspaper industry took off and helped to remake American journalism.

The earliest newspaper in New York was William Bradford's *New York Gazette,* which began in 1725; it was Bradford's former partner, John Peter Zenger, who—after founding a new paper, the *New-York Weekly Journal*—would make history in 1735 when he was tried and acquitted on charges of "seditious libel," in a case that would help establish the principle of freedom of the press. And one of New York's most famous citizens, Alexander Hamilton, was responsible in 1801 for the founding of the *New-York Evening Post,* which is still in business today. But newspapers did not truly become big business in New York until the advent of the

BELOW This 1936 photograph by Berenice Abbott shows the land between Broadway, Park Row, and Chambers Street now known as City Hall Park. A public space since the 1600s, it is best known for the media industry. Left to right: Pulitzer Building, Tribune Building, Times Building, and Potter Building.

"penny press" in the 1830s, with the number of daily newspapers soaring to 35 in that decade, including such names as the *Herald* and the *Sun*, followed soon by the *Tribune* and the *Times*, among many others.

As the city expanded across the nineteenth century, becoming not only much larger but also far more diverse, the public's appetite for news—and for sensationalism—grew alongside it. So did printing technology, enabling the use of more sophisticated graphics and the advent of lavish, and often lurid,

illustrations. Many of these were under the aegis of the competing media empires of Hungarian immigrant Joseph Pulitzer, who purchased the *New York World* in 1883, and of displaced Californian and perennial political hopeful William Randolph Hearst, whose *Morning Journal* and other papers were credited with stirring up American sentiment in favor of war against Spain in 1898. This so-called "yellow journalism" appealed to popular tastes, championed social reform, and offered a dubious mix of genuine reporting

and sensationalism. They were joined by a variety of foreign-language and political newspapers that found an eager audience in specialized markets in the city.

By the middle of the twentieth century, there were a dozen English-language newspapers published daily in Manhattan, and the hardboiled reporter had become one of the classic New York "types." But the advent of a new medium—also born in New York—changed everything. Television, pioneered by the American Telephone & Telegraph Company (AT&T) in the 1920s, had become a consumer item at the end of the 1930s, with early broadcasts including the 1939 World's Fair in the newly built Flushing Meadows in Queens and a college baseball game that same year. Soon New York City was home to four television networks—ABC, CBS, NBC, and the DuMont network—and the location of the studios that created most of the live programming broadcast across the country.

Television opened the door for the coming of age of another quintessentially New York industry—advertising. New York's newspapers, street corners, and radio airwaves had been saturated with ads for decades, but the new medium unleashed new creative potential and dollars. In the 1960s, the era immortalized in the twenty-first-century television series "Mad Men,"—Madison Avenue's advertising firms, including such giants as Doyle Dane Bernbach, Ogilvy & Mather, and Young & Rubicam, launched a series of creative campaigns that left their mark on American culture as well as American consumerism. Among their campaigns were "Think Small" for Volkswagen, and "You Don't Have to Be Jewish to Love Levy's," for the New York-based bakery, helping to turn advertising itself not only into big business, but into what some have called the quintessential twentieth-century art form.

LEGENDARY CAMPAIGNS

Victor Talking Machine Co., "His master's voice,"
Francis Barraud, 1901
Featuring a fox-terrier, this ad would become a world-wide icon.

Coca-Cola, "The pause that refreshes,"
D'Arcy Co., 1929
This iconic ad portrayed Coca-Cola as a "pleasant interlude in everyday life."

Maidenform, "I dreamed I went shopping in my Maidenform bra," Norman, Craig & Kunnel, 1949
Brazen for its time, this ad featured a half-naked woman in a dream-scenario, content in her undergarments.

Burger King, "Have it your way," BBDO, 1973
This ad and jingle campaign aimed to highlight Burger King's "flexibility."

Hathaway Shirts, "The man in the Hathaway shirt," Hewitt, Ogilvy, Benson & Mather, 1951
The first of this mysterious ad series ran in The New Yorker for only $3,176; by week's end, Hathaway shirts were sold out.

Clairol, "Does she...or doesn't she?" Foote, Cone & Belding, 1957
Penned by Shirley Polykoff, a Brooklyn mother, this titillating ad increased sales by 413% in just six years.

New York's Finest and Bravest

ABOVE New York City police officers, 1891.

In 1658, five years after New Amsterdam had secured its city charter, Director General Petrus Stuyvesant took formal steps to address threats to public safety. He implemented a "Rattle Watch" composed of eight citizens whose duty was to patrol the streets from 9 p.m. until morning drumbeat, calling out the time by the hour at all street corners and staying alert for fires. After the English assumed command in 1664, a military watch supplanted the Rattle Watch. A series of military and civilian watches prevailed in the ensuing years.

Fire was a far more significant problem than crime until well into the nineteenth century. The citizens' bucket brigades of the New Amsterdam and early English colonial periods proved sadly deficient. The city ordered its first fire truck from England in 1731: a goose-neck hand pumper, invented by Richard Newsham, with a wooden tank that required filling by a bucket brigade. Seven or eight men, working the brakes on either side

of the tank, forced water through the air pump into a goose-neck attached to a nozzle to create a spray of water that could reach much higher than water thrown by bucket. The hand pumper was pulled by men rather than by horses, and since a lot of men were needed, the city established its first volunteer fire department in 1737. New York's wealthiest and most noted citizens considered it an honor to belong to a fire company, and the romance of the brave fireman was the stuff of legend and song.

Manhattan's famous "grid plan" above 14th Street was adopted in 1811, born in part out of the necessity of preventing fires from spreading across narrow, crooked streets, as well as to facilitate future building. This grid plan, also known as the Commissioners' Plan, was the result of a New York State initiative to regularize Manhattan's avenues and streets. The need for the grid plan was starkly revealed in the devastating Great Fire of December 16–17, 1835, which damaged more property than any other event in the history of the city. Some 674

OPPOSITE A major fire at the notorious Tombs prison in Lower Manhattan broke out in 1842. John C. Colt, brother of Samuel Colt, inventor of the revolver, had been convicted of murder and scheduled to die at the seven-year-old city prison on November 18, 1842. The day before his hanging, he married his girlfriend and then pre-empted the hangman by stabbing himself in the heart. In the confusion that followed discovery of the suicide, a lamp or candle was knocked over, triggering a fire that destroyed the building's cupola and portions of the roof.

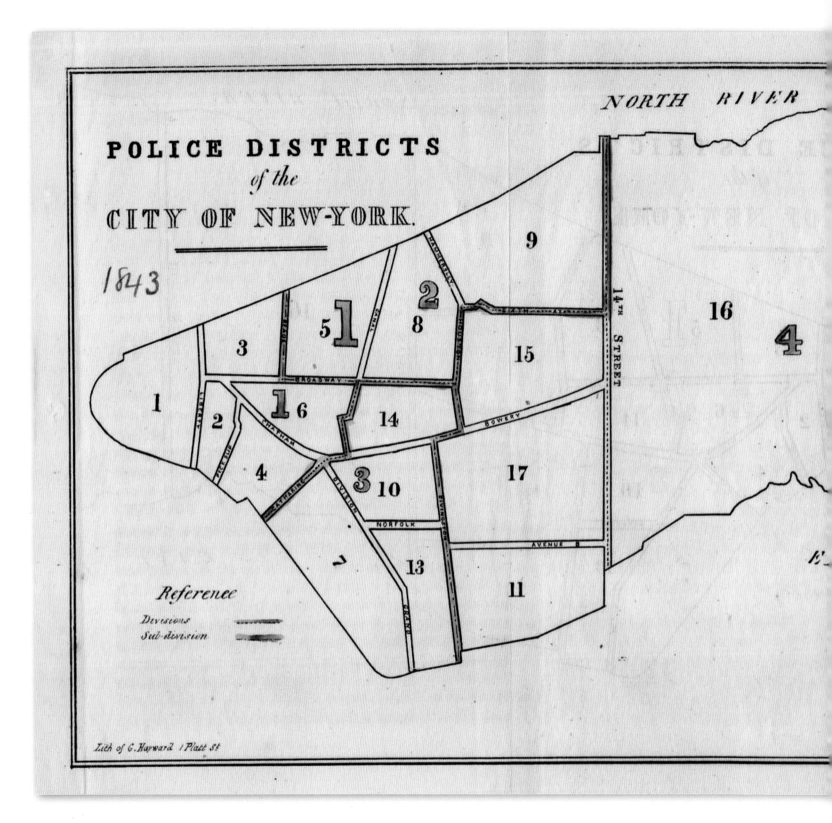

POLICE DISTRICTS
of the
CITY OF NEW-YORK.

1843

NORTH RIVER

Reference

Divisions

Sub-division

Lith of G. Hayward 1 Platt St

buildings were destroyed in more than 20 square blocks.

In the aftermath of the Great Fire, there were loud calls for the reorganization of the volunteer fire department and the introduction of a paid firefighting force. But the 4,000-strong, politically powerful and often unruly volunteer fire companies managed to stave off this change for 30 years.

By the middle of the nineteenth century, the fire companies were also, in effect, social and political clubs

populated by working-class men. For example, William M. Tweed, the famous "Boss" Tweed of Tammany Hall, the Democratic political club, actually began his career by being elected foreman of the Americus "Big Six" engine company in 1850. (The engine's tank was decorated with the head of a snarling tiger, which the political cartoonist Thomas Nast eventually adopted as a symbol for Tammany Hall.) Not until 1865, with the introduction of horse-drawn steam fire engines, did the end come for New

ABOVE Note that the northern boundary of the City of New York at the time this police map was made in about 1843 was 14th Street in Lower Manhattan. At the time, city officials were working to reorganize and professionalize the police force. Two years later, in 1845, Mayor William F. Havemeyer established

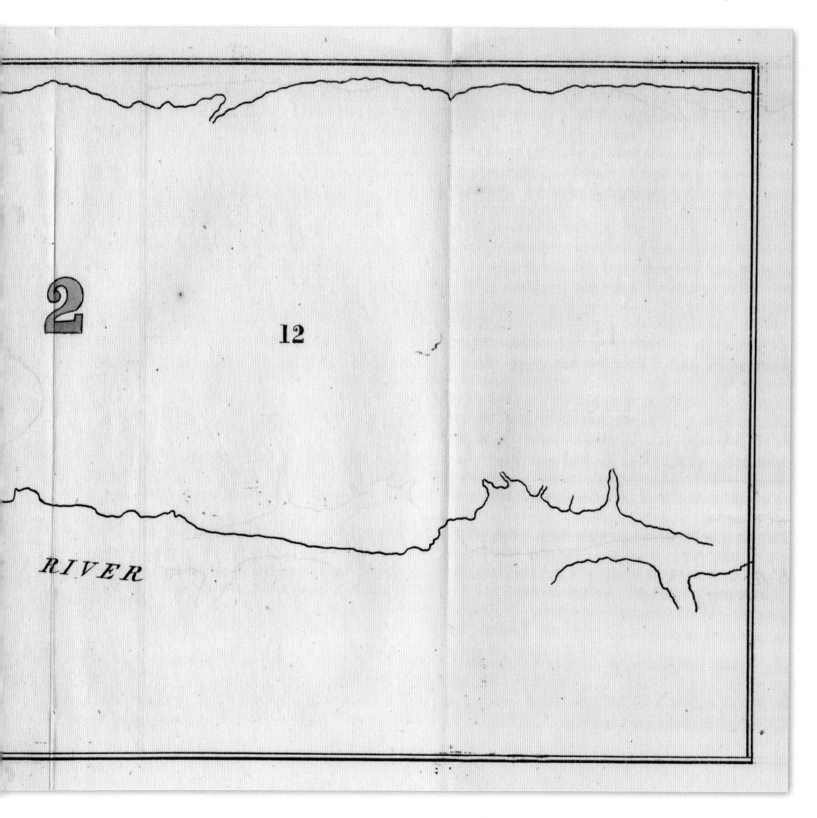

2

12

RIVER

a "Day and Night" police force of as many as 800 men who were identified by star-shaped badges.

York City's volunteer fire department. A new Metropolitan Fire Department, deploying 700 paid firemen in stations across Manhattan and Brooklyn, replaced the volunteers. The first motorized fire trucks came into use in the 1920s; the last run of a horse-drawn fire truck was in 1922.

Crime, meanwhile, seemed to spike at times but to follow a less treacherous course. The city established a police force in 1783 to counteract the chaos after the American Revolution, and an administrative structure was in place by 1800. By 1818, Mayor Cadwallader Colden reported that crime was low and infractions minor. But the influx of immigrants, the growing disparity between rich and poor, and the rise of gangs contributed to a new momentum of crime in the 1820s. Riots threatened the city throughout the 1830s, underscoring the inadequacy of the policing system and the paramount need for reform. By the Municipal Police Act of 1845, the mayor of New York City assumed control and created

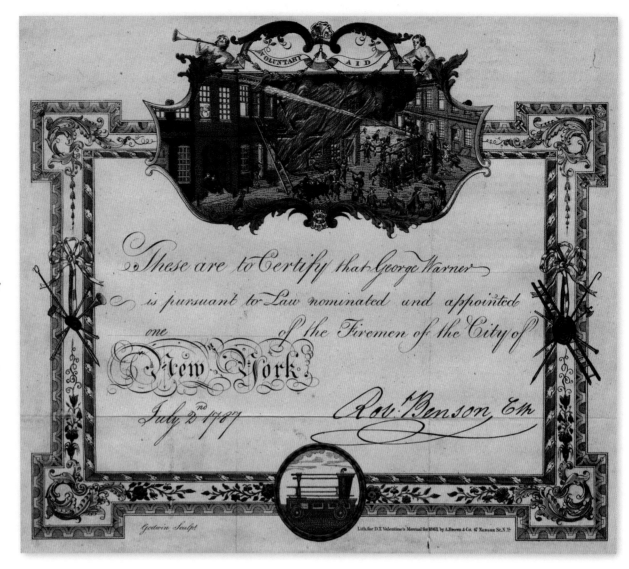

a London-style police force (one staffed by a full-time, professional force of crime preventers) for the first time.

The force soon succumbed to tensions with the new populations, uneven distribution among wards, patronage, and corruption. In 1857, the New York State legislature declared that the city was too corrupt to govern itself and by means of the Metropolitan Police Act transferred the responsibility for police protection from municipal to state authorities. New York City Mayor Fernando Wood resisted this effort at state control, and for a time the city had dueling police forces. The state eventually prevailed in the courts. The Metropolitan police force distinguished themselves in quelling the 1863 Draft Riot, but the postwar demoralization of the city, an increase in crime, and the force's failure to achieve administrative stability or public acceptance led to its eventual demise. The Metropolitans were abolished in 1870 and replaced by a Police Department controlled by the City.

Crime ebbed and surged in the following years, often in direct relationship to the level of corruption in the New York City Police Department (NYPD), whose self-proclaimed nickname is "New York's Finest." Corruption was especially rampant in the 1890s. In 1895, reform mayor William L. Strong appointed Theodore Roosevelt police commissioner. Roosevelt proceeded to

purge the force of corrupt leadership, demand discipline and efficiency in the ranks, and enforce the closing of saloons on Sundays. He also conducted nightly inspection patrols around the city with the reform journalist and photographer Jacob Riis.

The twentieth century saw the further professionalization of New York's police force. Although charges of corruption surfaced at key moments—especially during Prohibition in the 1920s and in the 1970s—City and State officials regularly implemented reforms. In the 1960s and 70s, Mayor John Lindsay expanded the force, fought (unsuccessfully) for civilian review of complaints against officers, and implemented a controversial policy of police restraint. Mayor David Dinkins also expanded the force and crime began to fall. The decline accelerated dramatically under his successor, Mayor Rudolph Giuliani, who put emphasis on quality-of-life crimes, although tensions arose over charges of overzealous policing and incidents of police brutality. The NYPD continues to seek to improve its relationship with the community and to become more representative of the city it is charged with protecting, while continuing to work to face the new and complex challenges of the twenty-first century as "New York's finest."

THE HEROISM OF 9/11

When American Airlines Flight 11 slammed into the North Tower of the World Trade Center on the morning of September 11, 2001, the members of the New York City Fire Department (FDNY) and New York Police Department (NYPD) sprang into action. They gave little thought to their safety; it was their mission to save the trapped people. On that one day, 23 New York City police officers, 37 members of the Port Authority police, and 343 firemen gave their lives—including every single member of the emergency response divisions of all five boroughs. Until that day, perhaps 800 members of the New York City Fire Department and its predecessor, the Metropolitan Fire Department, had died in the line of duty in the city's entire history.

LEFT A rescue worker walks through the debris at "Ground Zero" after the destruction of the World Trade Center on September 11, 2001. Firemen and other rescue workers became universally admired heroes as a result of their extraordinary efforts on that fateful day.

Making a Splash

"If you can make it here, you'll make it anywhere" may be a cliché, but it has been a mantra for generations of performers, extroverts, publicity hounds, and all of those seeking the glow of New York's limelight.

With its potent nexus of money, theater, society, and media, the city provides the perfect stage for grabbing headlines worldwide. Careers and reputations are created—and sometimes tested or destroyed—in the city's bright lights.

As early as the nineteenth century, New York was an almost mandatory stop for dignitaries, and New Yorkers learned to turn out in style to honor them. Among the visiting celebrities was the Marquis de Lafayette, a French hero of the American Revolution, whose return in 1824 was feted with parades, balls,

BELOW Confetti and tickertape rain down on the *Apollo 11* astronauts as they take part in a parade down Broadway to City Hall in celebration of their successful space flight and Moon landing the previous month, August 3, 1969.

receptions, banquets, and fireworks. The Prince of Wales got a similarly enthusiastic reception in 1860. Possibly the grandest reception of the pre-Civil War era was the 1860 welcome given to the first Japanese delegation to visit the West. New Yorkers treated their exotic visitors to a two-week whirlwind of parades, balls, and official tours, and the ambassadors, including the teenage interpreter nicknamed "Tommy," became instant celebrities, their every move the object of lavish press attention. Parades up lower Broadway, through what is today called the Canyon of Heroes, became popular in the late nineteenth century, with ticker tape from stock ticker machines being showered from above. (In recent history, since the demise of the stock ticker, confetti has been used instead.) Among those who have been so honored are Albert Einstein (1921), Charles Lindbergh (1927), the *Apollo 11* astronauts (1969), Pope John Paul II (1979), Nelson Mandela (1990), and countless others, including championship sports teams and returning veterans.

The power of New York's media, of course, is not to be underestimated in the city's role as publicity machine. Impresario Florenz Ziegfeld understood that perfectly in creating the reputation of Anna Held, his newfound star (and paramour)—well in advance of her first setting foot on a New York stage in 1896—by carefully feeding stories about her to the New York press. The public interest in Jenny Lind, the "Swedish Nightingale," had risen to a fever pitch by the time she made her heralded appearance at the Castle Garden Theater in 1850, although few Americans had heard of her before P. T. Barnum, who produced the tour, began

issuing releases to the New York press. One hundred years later, the Beatles' appearance on New York's *Ed Sullivan Show* was literally the stuff of which legends are made. Given the national reach of New York's media, particularly in the twentieth century, it is no surprise that stars seeking the spotlight sought to secure their place in the firmament by appearing in New York City.

Then there are the legends of New York society. As early as the 1840s, the city's "ins" and "outs" were publicly named by Moses Yale Beach, the publisher of the *New York Sun*, who began putting out annual lists of the city's wealthiest families. Major events of the social season were avidly followed from the days when Sarah Livingston Jay, wife of the statesman John Jay, became the city's legendary hostess. The names of the expected guests at such landmark social events as the Lafayette Ball (1824), the Prince of Wales Ball (1860), or the lavishly costumed Bradley Martin Ball (1897), were published for all to see and pore over. After the Civil War, wealth generated by the industrial revolution created vast new fortunes for some; however, sometimes these "new" families found themselves shut out of society events that were dominated by old New York families. (Samuel) Ward McAllister, a lawyer and society figure, prepared an exclusive guest list for Mrs William Astor, the wealthy socialite, which he labeled "The Four Hundred." This provided a platform for wealthy families to get their names in the papers by staging ever more lavish parties. The tradition of the major society event faded with the nineteenth century and the emergence of the more artistic—and more diverse—café society of the twentieth, but it was periodically reincarnated with

The Bradley Martin Ball — February 10, 1897

headline-grabbing events such as Truman Capote's glittering Black and White Ball in the Grand Ballroom of the Plaza Hotel in 1966.

But it is the stars themselves who really shine. As E.B. White wrote, there are many kinds of New Yorkers, but the most important are those who come to the city "willing to be lucky." Many of them have gained fame in the city that never sleeps and thus have become nearly synonymous with it: the artist Andy Warhol, who was living proof that far more than 15 minutes of fame could be obtained in the city; the boxer Sugar Ray Robinson and his unmistakable pink Cadillac; and snappy dressers from "Diamond" Jim Brady to Mae West and P. Diddy. And at the end of the day, fame is available to anyone ready to stake a place for themselves in the city: after all, what better place than Times Square to stand in your underwear and play the guitar with a cowboy hat on, as the Naked Cowboy does every day, making himself one of the countless New York characters who have used the city to make their own splash.

ABOVE Cornelia Sherman Martin and Bradley Martin (the Bradley-Martins) were known for lavish entertaining. On February 10, 1897, they hosted a masquerade ball at the Waldorf-Astoria, on a theme of the sixteenth, seventeenth, and eighteenth centuries. Hoping to stimulate the depressed local economy, they were criticized for excesses.

EVELYN NESBIT

Sometimes celebrity can take an unexpected turn. On June 25, 1906, one of New York's most notorious murder cases centered around a love triangle that included a showgirl, a multimillionaire, and one of the most celebrated architects of his time. Evelyn Nesbit, known for her provocative act as the "Girl on the Red Velvet Swing," married millionaire Harry Thaw. But when Thaw learned of his wife's earlier liaison with Stanford White of the firm McKim, Mead & White, architects of Grand Central Terminal, Pennsylvania Station, and the Morgan Library, he confronted White in a jealous rage and shot him three times at point-blank range. Thaw offered a plea of temporary insanity and attempted escape multiple times. Ultimately, he was allowed to go free after having been deemed sane. Nesbit did not fare so well; several suicide attempts, divorce, and a failed reconciliation with Thaw left her with a lifelong struggle to control her alcoholism and resurrect her once successful career.

LEFT Evelyn Nesbit, as photographed by Arnold Genthe in 1916, a decade after the shooting of her former lover, Stanford White, in the "crime of the century."

Cultural Institutions

Today, New York has more than 150 museums, from the Alice Austen House to the Yeshiva University Museum, including some of the greatest cultural institutions in the world. But the story of the creation of many of the city's most famous museums, which draw people from around the globe to experience the art, culture, history, science, and natural history of the world in one metropolis, was the work of a relatively small group of people fairly late in the city's history.

Early isolated efforts to create cultural resources occurred shortly after Independence. The oldest existing museum in New York is the New-York Historical Society. It was created in 1804 to preserve the history of the colonial and revolutionary periods, whose records and memories, its founders feared, were being lost in the forward rush of the developing city. Along with the National Academy of Design (1826) and the short-lived Lyceum of Natural History (1817), the Society initiated the important process of assembling collections that shaped the cultural and intellectual character of the city. However, many nineteenth-century "museums" in New York, as

Historical Museums

⑩ THE AMERICAN NUMISMATIC SOCIETY
Broadway between 155th and 156th Streets
COINS, medals and decorations of all countries and periods, emphasis being placed on those of the United States. An exceptionally complete library.
Daily and Sundays 2-5. Free. (Library closed Sundays.)

④ HALL OF FAME FOR GREAT AMERICANS
New York University ... University Heights at 181st Street
AN open air colonnade honoring America's famous men and women who are commemorated by bronze tablets and portrait busts by contemporary American sculptors.
Daily, Sundays and holidays 8:30-dusk. Free.

⑪ MUSEUM OF THE AMERICAN INDIAN
Heye Foundation ... Broadway at 155th Street
COMPREHENSIVE collection pertaining to ethnology and archæology of the Indians from North, South and Central Americas and the West Indies. (Stays open Summer 1939).
Daily 2-5. Closed Sundays and holidays. Free.

⑭ MUSEUM OF THE CITY OF NEW YORK
Fifth Avenue at One Hundred and Fourth Street
THE aim of the Museum is to illustrate by means of exhibits the chronological development of the various phases of New York City life from earliest times to the present.
Daily 10-5; Sundays 1-5. Closed Tuesdays. Free except Mondays (25c).

⑬ MUSEUM OF JEWISH CEREMONIAL AND HISTORICAL OBJECTS
Jewish Theological Seminary of America, Broadway at 122nd Street
RELIGIOUS and ceremonial objects, historical documents, from Europe, Asia, Africa and America. Paintings, tapestries, embroideries. Illuminated manuscripts.
Daily and Sundays 10-5. Closed Fridays, Saturdays. Free.

⑬ AMERICAN JEWISH HISTORICAL SOCIETY
Broadway at One Hundred and Twenty-Second Street
RARE books, documents, portraits, objects of art illustrating the history of the Jews on the American continent.
Daily and Sundays 10-5. Closed Fridays, Saturdays. Free.

⑱ THE NEW YORK HISTORICAL SOCIETY
Central Park West, between Seventy-Sixth and Seventy-Seventh Streets
COLLECTIONS of American portraits, old New York views and relics. Folk Art, Audubon water colors of birds, Rogers group and European paintings.
Daily 10-5; Sundays and holidays, 1-5. Closed Mondays, New Year's Day, July Fourth, Thanksgiving and Christmas. Free.

㉞ THE SUB-TREASURY MUSEUM
Sub-Treasury Building ... Wall and Nassau Streets
WASHINGTON was inaugurated on this site. Exhibits are designed to re-create historical background of old New York.
Daily 10-4. Free.

㊲ STATEN ISLAND HISTORICAL SOCIETY
Court and Center Streets, Richmond, S. I.
COMMUNITY historical museum. Collections portray life of Staten Island—social, economic, political. Household articles and tools as well as finer material. Library.
Daily 9-5. Sundays and holidays 2-5. Free.

Science Museums

⑨ AMERICAN GEOGRAPHICAL SOCIETY
Broadway at One Hundred and Fifty-Sixth Street
SPECIAL exhibits of rare and unusual maps open to the public 2-5 every day except Mondays and Thursdays.
Library and map room open to qualified consultants daily 9-4:45. Closed Sundays and holidays. Free.

⑰ THE AMERICAN MUSEUM OF NATURAL HISTORY
Central Park West at Seventy-Ninth Street
ANIMALS of the plains and jungles of Asia and Africa—many in their natural environment. Finest collection of fossil reptiles in the world. Mastodons, mammoths. Exquisite jades, gems. Cultures of various races of man.
Daily 10-5; Sun., Jan. 1, Jul. 4, Thanksgiving, Christmas, 1-5. Free.

㊳ THE BROOKLYN CHILDREN'S MUSEUM
Brooklyn Avenue and Park Place
SUPERVISED recreational and school education in natural sciences, history, geography and crafts, utilizing exhibits, libraries, studios, work shops and field trips.
Daily 10-5; Sundays 2-5. Free.

⑰ HAYDEN PLANETARIUM
Central Park West at Eighty-First Street
"IN the Planetarium, the Theater of the Stars, the stage is the whole of creation, the actors the bright celestial objects of vast, even inconceivable, space and time."
Performances (to Nov. 1, 1939): Weekdays, hol. 11, 1-5, 8, 9. Sun. 2-5, 8, 9. Adults, 25c morning and afternoon; 35c evening; Children 15c.

㉒ NEW YORK MUSEUM OF SCIENCE AND INDUSTRY
RCA Building ... Rockefeller Center
SCIENCE in action. The marvels of electricity; wonders of modern communication and transportation; progress of mankind in housing, food, textiles, machinery, power; shown in exhibits most of which the visitor may operate.
Daily and Sundays 10-10. Adults 25c, Children 10c.

㊲ STATEN ISLAND INSTITUTE OF ARTS AND SCIENCES
Stuyvesant Place and Wall Street, St. George, S. I.
COLLECTIONS relating especially to Staten Island. Plants, animals, minerals, Indian relics, genealogical records, art exhibits, reference library.
Daily 10-5; Sundays 2-5. Free.

Issued July 1939
The above information is subject to change without notice.

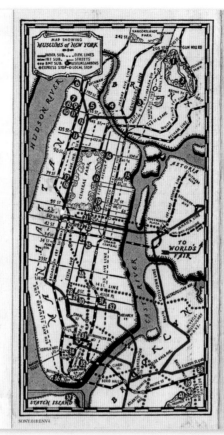

MUSEUMS
OF NEW YORK

Including

HISTORIC HOUSES, BOTANICAL
AND ZOOLOGICAL GARDENS
and THE AQUARIUM

These museums offer opportunity for recreation, for study, for pleasure, and for greater understanding of the world in which we live.

MUSEUMS COUNCIL
OF NEW YORK CITY
Secretary's Office:
NEW YORK MUSEUM OF SCIENCE AND INDUSTRY
R. C. A. BUILDING ... ROCKEFELLER CENTER

---

elsewhere in the country, were motley collections of artifacts and curiosities, as much sideshows as museums. Appropriately, the most famous of these "dime museums" was run by none other than impresario and showman Phineas T. Barnum. In 1841, three decades before opening the world's first three-ring circus, Barnum created the American Museum in Lower Manhattan. His museum staged such acts as "General Tom Thumb" and Jenny Lind (the "Swedish Nightingale"), foisted hoaxes such as the "Feejee Mermaid" on the public, and showcased scientific curiosities and artifacts from around the world.

The watershed moment for the city's cultural life came right after the Civil War. In the last third of the nineteenth century, a group of civic leaders declared that New York needed a world-class cultural life to match its growing economic power as well as its position as a truly international city. Determined that the city shed its reputation as a cultural backwater, and funded with fortunes accumulated by New York industrialists during and after the war, the extraordinarily energetic and productive Andrew Haswell Green drove the move to provide city land and build glorious buildings on the perimeter of Central Park for the American Museum of the Natural History (1869) and the Metropolitan Museum of Art (1880). Not to be outdone, the City of Brooklyn erected a new building for the Brooklyn Institute (1897, now the Brooklyn Museum) on Eastern

Parkway, while Staten Island created the Staten Island Institute of Arts and Science (1881).

The twentieth century saw the dizzying transformation of New York City into a modern, multicultural city, and with it a new rush of cultural institutions. Responding to a city that had been drastically remade as a result of immigration and development, the founders of the Museum of the City of New York (1923) had a twofold purpose for their institution: to teach the legions of new arrivals about their adopted hometown and to preserve the history of New York. A particular focus was given to the preservation of the contents of historic homes that were being torn down to make way for new corporate development. As the first museum in the United States dedicated to the study of a single city, it amassed a collection of photographs, prints, paintings, costumes, decorative arts, and theatrical memorabilia, quickly becoming a repository for the documentation of the evolution of New York City's people, politics, and built environment.

The years between the world wars also saw the creation of institutions exhibiting and promoting the work of modern and contemporary art. The Museum of Modern Art (1929), the Whitney Museum of American Art (1930), and the Museum of Non-Objective Painting (1939, now the Solomon R. Guggenheim Museum) all encouraged the appreciation of an evolving cultural climate. After the Second World War, the growing

momentum of historic preservation led to a proliferation of historic site museums such as Richmond Town Restoration on Staten Island (1958), the Wyckoff House Museum in Queens (1967), and Staten Island's Snug Harbor Cultural Center (1976), among many others.

The middle and late twentieth century saw a proliferation of arts and history organizations that reflected the diversity and changing dynamics of New York City. The Jewish Museum (1947), the Studio Museum in Harlem (1967), El Museo del Barrio (1969), the Museum of Chinese in America (1980), and the Lower East Side Tenement Museum (1988), are just a few of the museums dedicated to the diverse peoples of New York. The many faces of contemporary art are reflected in such entities as the PS 1 Contemporary Art Museum (1971), the Bronx Museum of the Arts (1971), the Queens Museum (1972), the New Museum of Contemporary Art (1977), and many, many more.

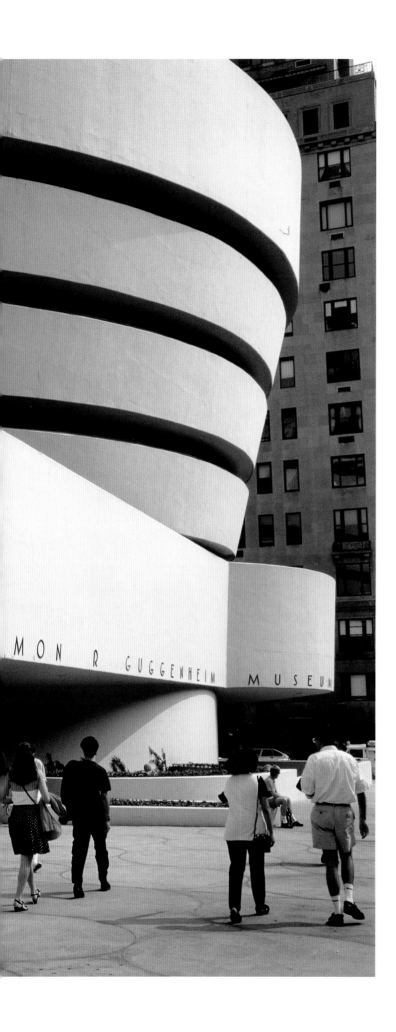

THE GUGGENHEIM

Iconic in stature and boldly different from the surrounding architecture, Frank Lloyd Wright's commission is one of his most identifiable buildings and a landmark of post-Second World War architecture, situated on Fifth Avenue on New York's museum mile. In 1943, Solomon R. Guggenheim commissioned Wright to design a permanent structure for his collection of twentieth-century art. Wright soon landed on a unique concept, though it would go through numerous iterations over the next fifteen years: a white, reinforced concrete structure spiraling skyward that increased in size from the base, forming an inverted cone. The interior, with its massive multistory atrium, allows uninterrupted sight lines throughout the main exhibition space. A gentle, spiraling ramp provides for a relatively unbroken installation of the collection. The project initially received negative comments, yet became a symbol of American architectural innovation. The great irony of the structure is that neither Wright nor Guggenheim lived to see its completion.

LEFT The Solomon R. Guggenheim Museum, on Fifth Avenue at 89th Street, was designed by the great Frank Lloyd Wright and completed in 1959. Within its iconic spiral architecture, modern masterpieces from the twentieth century and beyond are displayed in particularly viewer-friendly fashion.

OPPOSITE The Whitney Museum of American Art, on Madison Avenue near 75th Street, specializes in American art of the twentieth and twenty-first centuries.

A Modern Melting Pot

New York City is home to more than 8,250,000 people, making it the most populous city in the United States by far. In fact, four of the city's five boroughs, if considered as separate cities, would rank in the top ten US cities by population. Where do all these people come from? To a remarkable extent, they come from abroad. More than three million, or 37 percent, are foreign-born. Together, first- and second-generation New Yorkers account for almost two-thirds of the city's population.

Indeed, immigration to New York is proceeding at a pace not seen in close to a century. (In 2010, New York City's foreign-born population was beginning to approach the twentieth-century high of 40 percent in 1910.) And, if the newcomers of today rival those of the past in sheer numbers, they far exceed them in the diversity of their origins. A century and-a-half ago, immigrants to New York came primarily from Europe; today they come from throughout the world—from no fewer than 100 nations, in fact, according to the 1990 census—and speak more than 120 languages, from Armenian to Vietnamese.

This diversity dates from major changes in US immigration laws in the 1960s, when the Hart-Cellar Act (the Immigration and Nationality Act) of 1965 lifted the restrictions that had been in place on immigration since 1924, and opened New York's doors anew to mass immigration and a far greater diversity of nationalities than ever before in the city's history. Newcomers from Asia, Latin America, and the Caribbean soon far outnumbered those from countries that had traditionally seen an exodus. Dominican and other Hispanic immigrants followed in the footsteps of Puerto Ricans, who, as US citizens, had begun a mass migration to New York following the Second World War. Within 25 years, New York's foreign-born population had jumped from 18 percent to 39 percent. Heavy multinational immigration shows no sign of abating in the twenty-first century.

As in the past, the newest immigrants tend to congregate in neighborhoods where their compatriates have settled. The established Little Germany (better known as Kleindeutschland) and Little Italy have been joined by Little Africa, not to mention a very Little Sri Lanka (on

BELOW This view, entitled "Chinese Writing–Canal Street," was captured in 1981 by Andreas Feininger, at a time when Canal Street was considered the northern border of Chinatown. Today, signs in Chinese–as well as in Vietnamese, Malay, and many other Asian languages–can be seen throughout the neighborhoods of Little Italy and the Lower East Side. Manhattan's Chinatown still has the highest Chinese population of any in the nation, but new Chinatowns have also emerged in Brooklyn and Queens.

Staten Island). In a city of diverse boroughs, Queens stands out: almost half its residents are foreign-born, and dozens of its neighborhoods have been transformed by waves of Chinese, Haitians, Arabs, Mexicans, South Americans, and South and Southeast Asians, among others, making it the most diverse place in the United States.

Yet Queens is hardly alone. Every borough has a critical mass of first- or second-generation immigrants. The city's population of Spanish speakers is so large that most non-Hispanic officials make a point of peppering their speeches with a Spanish words and phrases. In the city's public schools—whose register of 1.1 million students exceeds the entire population of eight US states—documents such as registrations, report cards, and system-wide alerts are routinely translated into Spanish, French, German, Chinese, Japanese, Urdu, Persian, Hindi, Russian, Bengali, Haitian Creole, Korean, and Arabic.

How do they all get along? As a rule, very well. The city's size and ethnic diversity allows immigrants to find safety and comfort in ethnic enclaves and yet also to venture out of those enclaves to work, to go to school, and to encounter people of vastly different backgrounds and experiences. The city is large enough to support countless subcultures. Some younger South Asian New Yorkers—American-born Indians, Pakistanis, Bangladeshis, Sri Lankans, and Nepalese, plus the

so-called twice or thrice immigrants, such as Indo-Caribbeans—have even created a new identity: Desi, a Sanskrit word that means "of my country."

Of course, New York's great experiment in diversity is not always trouble-free. While it is not uncommon for one national group to live in peaceful proximity to another group who would be their enemy back home, the process of ethnic succession—especially for neighborhoods fabled for harboring one nationality—can be fraught, though rarely violently so. New Yorkers are no less likely than non-New Yorkers to ascribe certain characteristics to certain nationalities—but on the whole, New Yorkers appreciate the value of immigration.

For whatever their feeling about particular groups, New Yorkers understand—in their bones, so to speak—that their city's strength rests largely on its ability to attract hard-working newcomers who bring energy and ideas, open small businesses, work long hours to make lives better for their children, send their children to school, pay their taxes, exercise their right to vote, and participate in the American Dream. The city even celebrates its heritage officially, with an annual Immigrant History Week each April, established in 2004 by Michael R. Bloomberg, the New York City mayor who has been one of the most energetic boosters of immigration in the city's history.

155

ETHNIC NEWSPAPERS

New York's media market is not only one of the largest in the world, but it is also one of the most diverse. Today, dailies are published in 42 languages and New York's ethnic press includes some 300 magazines and newspapers. New York's most broadly circulated Spanish-language daily, *El Diario La Prensa* (1963), is the oldest in America. *The Jewish Daily Forward*, a Jewish-American paper published bilingually in both Yiddish and English, started publication in 1897. In 1909, James Henry Anderson started the *African-American* weekly, *New York Amsterdam News*, in Harlem, which is still published today. Many other dailies serve the Korean, Polish, and Greek communities in the city and there are a number of papers addressed to New York's variety of religious communities. As the shifting density of cultural and ethnic groups in New York continually evolves, the number of equally diverse publications in the metropolis follows suit.

LEFT Although immigrants from Arab countries have been in New York since the late nineteenth century, significant immigration from the Arab world did not occur until after passage of the Hart-Cellar Act in 1965. Today Christians are in the majority among Arab New Yorkers, although a sizeable proportion of the second-wave immigrants are Muslim. Most live in Brooklyn, with a concentration in the neighborhood of Bay Ridge. In this 1999 photograph, Mel Rosenthal captured a Palestinian wedding at Widdi Catering Hall in Bay Ridge, with the bride and groom sitting at the head table while the groom's mother tries to keep the playing children from colliding with the elaborate wedding cake.

Index

Credits

The publishers would like to thank the following sources for their kind permission to reproduce the pictures in this book.

Key: t = Top, b = Bottom, c = Centre, l = Left, r = Right

Alamy Images: /Patrick Batchelder: **115**, /Martin Bond: **73t**, / Wendy Connett: **152**, /Ian Dagnall: **17**, /Historical Art Collection (HAC): **15**, / Richard Levine: **155**, /Patti McConville: **121**, /Stock Connection Blue: **153**, /NobleIMAGES: **86l**

Corbis: /Adam Stoltman: 119/Bettmann: **51**, /Condé Nast Archive: **131**, /Ewing Galloway: **112**, /Kelly Mooney Photography: **35b**, /Jose Fuste Raga: **5**, **80-81**, /Martin Roe/ Retna Ltd: **59**, /Michael Yamashita: **74-75**

Getty Images: /Steve Kelley: **65**, /Keystone/Hulton Archive: **6-7**, /Chris McGrath: **105**, /Michael Ochs Archives: **95**, / New York Daily News: **144**, Gilles Petard/Redferns : **101b**

PA Photos: /Eric Miller/AP: **93**

Photolibrary.com: /Alexander Poschel: **82**, /Visions LLC: **23**, /Barry Winiker: **118**

Rex Features: /Andrea Boohers: **142-143**, /Dan Callister: **65** , /Everett Collection: **135**, /Greg Mathieson: **57**

The Bridgeman Art Library: /Archives Charmet: **4**, /Ken Welsh: **33b**

Topfoto.co.uk: /The Granger Collection: 64, **123**, **/Curt Teich Postcard Archives/HIP: 73b**, **150**

Museum of the City of New York 2: *Liberty Enlightening the World* (Published by Root and Tinker, ca.1886), 29.100.1594; **3:** Medallic Art Co., World's Fair Medal Issued in Celebration of the 300th Anniversary of the Founding of the City of New York 1664–1964 (1964), 94.64.6AB; **6-7:** Samuel H. Gottscho, *From Roof of St. George Hotel* (1930), 88.1.5.82; **8:** *Manhattan Island Before the Dutch Settlement* (19th century), Print Archives; **9t:** Dutch cap (17th century), 2008.5.1; **9b:** Asher B. Durand, *Dance on the Battery in the Presence of Peter Stuyvesant* (1838), 55.248; **10:** Land patent (May 15, 1664), 33.307; **11:** Jacques Cortelyou, *The Castello Plan* (Map issued by Fratelli Alinari,1660), 31.227; **12:** William Winstanley, *George Washington*, 31.227; **13t:** Johannes A. Oertel, *Pulling Down the Statue of George III at the Bowling Green, City of New York, July 1776* (engraving issued by John C. McRae, 1859), 29.100.2337; **13b:** *Washington's Entry into New York: On the Evacuation of the City by the British, November 25th, 1783* (Lithograph issued by Currier & Ives, 1857), 57.100.127; **14-15:** Captain Davies, *A View of the Attack Against Fort Washington and Rebel Redouts near New York* (print issued by Max Jaffe, 1929 facsimile of 1776 original), 41.62.106A-B; **16-17:** *View of Liberty Street, N.Y. From Broadway to Greenwich St. South side* (Lithograph issued by W. Stephenson & Co.), 39.253.2; **18:** Anthony Imbert, *Erie Canal Celebration, New York* (1825), 49.415.1; 19: Papers Certifying that George Elliga Moore Is a Free Negro (1783), 41.133.1; **20-21:** Nicolino Calyo, *Burning of the Merchants' Exchange, New York, December 16th &17th, 1835* (1835), 57.100.24; **22:** *The Harbor of New York* (lithograph issued by Currier & Ives), 57.100.24; 24: Samuel H. Gottscho, *The Hudson River looking north from below the George Washington Bridge. Showing railroad tracks and the George Washington Bridge* (1932), 39.20.30; **25t:** Berenice Abbott, *Fulton Street Dock: Manhattan Skyline* (1935), 89.2.1.35; **25b:** Creamware jug (1802-1810), 86.75.2; 26t: Trade card – Clipper Ship "Cyclone" (ca. 1860), 46.62.10; **26b:** Fitz Henry Lane, *Clipper Ship "Sweepstakes"* (1853), M50.5; **27:** *The Clipper Ship "Cosmos"* (lithograph issued by Currier & Ives, 1883-1886), 56.300.256; **28r:** *On Murrays Hill* (Lithograph issued by N. Currier, 1842), 57.100.56; 28l: George P. Morris, Esquire, Broadside of *The Croton Ode* (1842), 40.94; **29:** Byron Company, *Communications, Marconi, Wireless Telegraph Inc.* (1899), 93.1.1.17322; 30-31 : *Brooklyn Bridge, 1883* (lithograph issued by A. Major), 29.100.1752; 31: Invitation to the Opening of the New York and Brooklyn Bridge (May 24, 1883), 35.104.4A; **32:** Byron Company, [Home of Thomas A. Edison.] (1907), 93.1.1.8799; **33t:** John Bachmann, *Bird's Eye View of the New York Crystal Palace and Environs* (1853), 29.100.2387; **34:** Byron Company, *Steerage – S.S. "Pennland", Red Star Line* (1893), 93.1.1.18432; **35t:** J. R. Brady, *Bnai Jeshurun Synagogue* (ca.1830), 29.100.1611; 36: Certificate of Naturalization (1922), Manuscript Collection; **37:** Jacob A. Riis, [Mulberry Street] (1900), 90.13.2.215; **38-39:** Jacob A. Riis, *Yard in Jersey Street (now gone) where Italians lived in the then worst slums.* (ca. 1897), 0.13.4.102; **40:** Byron Company, *Portrait, Richard Croker (Tammany Boss)* (1899), 93.1.1.8725; 41t: *Interior View of Tammany Hall, Decorated for The National Convention, July 4th, 1868* (lithograph issued by Jos. Shannon's Manual), 57.300.522; **41b:** George P. Hall and Son, [Tammany Hall] (ca. 1900), 92.53.71; 42: Tammany Society invitation (1904), Manuscript Collection; **43:** Sol Libsohn for the Federal Art Project, *First Avenue & 10th Street Market Opening* (1938), 43.131.6.20; 44: Front Page of the *New York Herald* (April 25, 1865), Manuscript Collection; **45:** Thomas Nast, *"What Are You Laughing At? To the Victor Belong the Spoils"* (print issued by *Harper's Weekly*, November 25, 1871), 99.124.2; **46:** Jacob A. Riis with R.H. Lawrence and H.G. Piffard, *Blackwell's Island: The Lock-step Penitentiary* (ca. 1890), 90.13.2.3; **47:** Jacob A. Riis with R.H. Lawrence and H.G. Piffard, *Police Headquarters, The "Rogue's Gallery"* (ca. 1890), 90.13.1.92; 48l: Deposition taken by Henry Abell, Watchman (August 10, 1824). 43.42.21; **48-49:** *Five Points, 1827* (print issued by Valentine's Manual, ca. 1850). 97.227.3; **50:** F. Coffey, *The Real Ellen* [sic] *Jewett* (print issued by Henry R. Robinson, 1836), 95.54.13; **52:** Byron Company, *Flag Factory, Making United States Flags* (1913), 93.1.1.4229; **53:** *Stuart's Steam Sugar Refinery* (ca.1850), 29.100.2117; **54:** Lewis Hine, *Empire State Building Construction* (ca. 1930), L638.8; **55:** Byron Company, *Labor Leaders: Samuel Gompers, John Burns, Holmes* (ca. 1893), 93.1.1.8917; **56:** James H. Cafferty, *Wall Street, Half Past 2 O'clock, Oct. 13, 1857*, 40.54; **58:** United States Office of War Information, *Stock Exchange* (1944). 90.28.17; 61t: Subway ticket (1904). 35.51.1; **61b:** Robert L. Bracklow, *Fifth Avenue Coach at Madison Square Park* (1900), 93.91.169; **62:** J.S. Johnston, *View of South Ferry and Elevated Railway* (1894), Print Archives; 63: Wurts Bros., *Interior of Penn Station, 1939*, X2010.7.1.12990; **66:** Edward Troye, *The American Eclipse* (1834), 95.54.1; **66-67:** Johannes A. Oertel, *Woodruff Stables* (1861), 34.340; **68:** Charles R. Parsons and Lymon Wetmore Atwater, *Summer Scenes in New York Harbor*, (lithograph issued by Currier & Ives, 1869), 57.300.47; **69:** Byron Company, *Sports, Bicycle Races, Manhattan Beach* (1896), 93.1.1.17486; **70:** Stansbury Norse, *Old Blockhouse in Central Park* (1888), 52.361; **71:** Johann Mongles Culverhouse, *Skating in Central Park* (1865), 29.100.1301; **72:** Samuel H. Gottscho, *Luna Park* (1906), 54.77.6; **76:** Byron Company, *Building, Automatic Vaudeville & Interiors (48 East 14th Street)* (ca. 1904), 93.1.1.1836; **77:** Sigismund de Ivanowski, *Ethel Barrymore as Madame Trentoni in Clyde Fitch's play, "Captain Jinks of the Horse Marines,"* 53.205; **78-79:** *Thomas D. Rice Performing "Jump, Jim Crow" Routine at American Theatre, Bowery, New York, Nov. 25th, 1833*, 32.483; **83:** Berenice Abbott *City Arabesque* (1938), 40.140.36AB; **84:** Wurts Bros., *Woolworth Building, watercolor rendering by Hughson Hawley* (ca. 1910), X2010.7.1.1360; **85:** Samuel H. Gottscho, *United Nations Building*, (1956), 56.323..46; **86-87:** Wurts Bros., [Skyline view showing Empire State Building] (ca. 1939), X2010.7.1.7562; **88:** Samuel H. Gottscho, *Forest Hills set. 16 Tower from [the] Green* (1927), 88.1.1.193; **89:** Victor Prevost, [The Woodlawn Hotel, Bronx] (1853-1854), 98.126.1.7; **90-91t:** Louisa Ann Coleman, *Winter Scene in Brooklyn, New York, 1817-20*, 53.2; **91b:** *Brooklyn Bridge Under Construction* (1881), Print Archives; 74l: Wurts Bros., *321-325 East 73rd Street. Bohemian National Hall* (ca. 1905), X2010.7.1.841; **94:** Jessie Tarbox Beals, *Down the Rabbit Hole, 150 West 4th – Greenwich Village* (ca. 1918), 95.127.9; **96-97:** Berenice Abbott, *Washington Square, Looking North* (1936), 43.131.1.144; **98:** Lithograph by Major and Knapp for *Valentines Manual. Harlem Lane from Central Park toward Manhattanville* (1865), Prints Collection.; **99:** [Hamilton Grange] (1897), X2010.11.1799; **100l:** Byron Company, *Amateur Productions, "Carolyn Capers, 1934,"* 93.1.1.20071; **101t:** Joseph Rodriguez, *Game of Skellie, East Harlem, 1987*, 2007.8.1; **102:** Jay Hambidge, *Crowd at the Polo Grounds* (print issued by the Truth Company, 1895), 42.111.2; **103:** Jacob A. Riis, *Boy's Ball Team in West Side playground* (ca. 1895), 90.13.2.150; **104:** Ebbets Field 1949 All Star Game commemorative pin, 87.97.37; 106-107: New York Ball Club, Official Score[book] (1892), Manuscript Collection; **108-109:** Fred Pansing, *Sampson and Schley Leading the Fleet into N.Y. Harbor, Aug. 20, 1898*, 82.68.20; **110:** *Company 'G', 7th regiment, New York City Draft Riots* (1863). 53.53.7; **111:** Byron Company, *Fifth Avenue and 25th Street* (1919), 93.1.1.18021; 113 Air Raid Instructions (1940s), Manuscript Collection; 114: Invitation to the Inauguration Ceremonies of the New Building of the Metropolitan Museum of Art (November 5, 1894), 80.167; **116:** United States Office of War Information, *Metropolitan Opera interior* (1944), 90.28.84; **117t:** *Colored Engravings for the People...* (Lithograph advertisement issued by N. Currier), 56.300.260; 117b: Souvenir program, groundbreaking for Philharmonic Hall at Lincoln Center (May 14, 1959), 97.41.21; **120:** [Interior of the Lotos Club.] (ca. 1910), X2010.11.6098; **122:** George C. Cox, *Walt Whitman* (1887), 40.146; **124:** Charles Frederick Worth, wedding dress in ivory and gold satin damask (1878), 32.249A-B; **125:** Louis Maurer, [Fashion Plate outside sewing store] (1870), 48.230.4; 126-127: *Bedell New York Fashions catalog, 1903–1904*, 39.564.31; **128-129:** Byron Company, *Joseph J. Keyser Co., 225 West 36th St., Interior, Dress Making Factory* (1920) 93.1.1.4097; **130:** Wurts Bros., *1530 Broadway. Bond Clothing Store, detail main entrance* (1941), 2010.7.1.8022; **132:** Berenice Abbott, *City Hall Park, "Newspaper Row"* (1936), 40.140.192; **133:** *Joseph Pulitzer* (ca. 1900), 41.132.74; **134:** Stanley Kubrick, [Television Show] (1946), LOOK Collection; **136:** Police (1891), X2010.11.11054; **137:** Albertis Del Orient Browere, *The Tombs Fire, 1842*, 29.100.1308; 138-139: *Police Districts of the City of New York* (ca. 1843). 55.377.5; **140:** Louis Maurer, *The American Fireman: Rushing to the Conflict* (lithograph issued by Currier & Ives, 1858), 56.300.6; 141: Firemen's Certificate of Appointment (1787), 33.146.4; **145:** *First Appearance of Jenny Lind in America: At Castle Garden September11th, 1850* (lithograph issued by N. Currier, 1850), 29.100.1871; **146:** H. McVickar, *The Bradley Martin Ball* (1897), 45.335.1; **147:** Arnold Genthe, *Evelyn Nesbitt (Mrs. E.N. Clifford)* (1916), X2010.383.676; **148:** *Broadway South from City Hall–Barnham's Museum* (ca. 1845), 29.100.1846; 149: *Museums of New York, 1939*, 98.52.15; **151:** Samuel H. Gottscho, [Museum of the City of New York] (ca. 1932), 34.443.1; **154:** Andreas Feininger. *Chinese Writing – Canal Street* (1981). 90.40.92; **156-157** Mel Rosenthal, [Scene from a Palestinian wedding – Bride and groom seated at table in front of wedding cake] (1999), 2006.37.36

Every effort has been made to acknowledge correctly and contact the source and/or copyright holder of each picture and Carlton Books Limited apologises for any unintentional errors or omissions which will be corrected in future editions of this book.